MW01688576

DON'T QUIT !

Uncovering The Hidden Challenges of Your Process To Fulfill Your Potential

Pastor Tony Smith

VMI PUBLISHING COMPANY
Baltimore, Maryland

Thank you for your support.

God Bless

DON'T QUIT !

Uncovering The Hidden Challenges of Your Process To Fulfill Your Potential

Pastor Tony Smith

All scripture quotations, unless otherwise indicated, are taken from the Holy Bible, New King James Version.

Please note that the New King James publishing style capitalizes certain pronouns in Scripture that refer to the Father, Son, and Holy Spirit, and may differ from some Bible publishers' styles.

This book is published by

VMI Publishing Company
807 E. 43rd Street
Baltimore, MD 21212
(410) 433-8066

Cover & Graphic Design: Glorious Designs
Photographs of Pastor Smith: Jim Berger Photography
Photography: Alex Bramwell, Mauro Bighin, Joy Miller- Agency: Dreamstime.com

This book is dedicated to my mother, Shirley Smith, and my grandmother, the late Mary McClain for all of their love, discipline, and encouragement, while inspiring me to be the best that I can be in God.

Their lives have motivated me not to quit!

*Acknowledgements*

I'd like to recognize some people in their efforts to support the vision and process of writing this book and who I am.

Special Thanks To:

My mother, Shirley Smith, my father, William Smith Sr., my son, Tony Smith Jr., his mother, Karen Smith, my brothers, Robert and William, and my niece Keisha.

Also to Lonnia McCargo, Eddie Jackson, Lenora Howze, Tiffany Watson, Kenneth Norris, Cheryl Hair, Tony Sawyer, Edwin Johnson, Gloria Handy, Juan Beverly, Marcy Clark, Chantal Wilson, Marcus Bevans, all of the leadership of Victory Ministries International, the entire family of Victory Ministries International, and all of my children in the spirit and brothers and sisters in the gospel.

If there is anyone I missed, I apologize and I want you to charge it to my mind and not to my heart!

Love You!

Contents

Introduction

Every living person has a purpose. With every person's purpose there is a process. This book will reveal the challenges that come out of your process on your way to fulfilling your purpose. My desire is to encourage you not to quit. Your purpose is already within you, but your process is planned outside of you. As you go through this book, I will uncover how the things that you rejected may have been the things you should have accepted. I find it amazing how many people never reach their full potential because they will not accept the road of their process to receive the fullness of their purpose.

You need to understand that God has already placed potential within you. It was there from the beginning. God doesn't go back and continue to add potential. Through His word, He has given you every bit of instruction and direction needed to discover and walk in your potential—if you don't reject your process.

In a relationship, there are certain criteria that need to be present in order to successfully develop and maintain a healthy and Godly intimate union. This book is created as a guide for men and women. I will show you the standards and principals that a man needs to possess to bring order in marriage, and also prepare the single reader of what to require in a relationship prior to marriage. These requirements are not a man-made formula to try to repair a relationship, but they are God's standards according to the Holy Bible.

I do want to warn you. In reaching your potential for your purpose, there will be some frustration during the process. Just like anything newly purchased, there is a period of adjustment and sometimes during that period of adjustment, you will run into errors and have to pull out the manual. The manual we will be using is God's word. Don't be afraid to continue because there are challenges. The best part about a challenge is the victory you gain after enduring the journey. Stay focused, and prepare yourself because the potential that God has personally placed within you is about to be pulled out, thus taking you to higher heights and deeper depths. If you've ever told yourself that you needed clarity in the area of your purpose, or ever felt that you have God-given potential but haven't yet discovered it, this book will empower you to obtain everything that God prepared for you to have. Enjoy the journey of reading this book as it exposes the process of reaching your potential and discovering your purpose.

1

It Was There In the Beginning

There are too many men, women, and children who are afraid to go forward in life because they don't think they have the potential. Afraid to move to a higher level because they don't think they have the potential. Afraid of walking into the full realization of their potential because they don't think they possess it. But, the potential was there in the beginning. Why haven't they reached full potential? Why have not we, the body of Christ reached our full potential? As far as potential is concerned, we have given our rights away. In this chapter, I will expose the potential that you are aware of, but never make use of. It's already within you. You already know about it and I am about to awaken it in you.

<u>Scripture point</u>: (Isaiah 46:8-9) "Remember this, and show yourselves men; Recall to mind, O, you transgressors. Remember the former things of old, for I am God, and there is no other; I am God, and there is none like Me,…. "

Do you know God? If you do, God is saying, remember who I am. If there was no "I am", there would be no "you". God is asking you to go back. Go back to the beginning of your relationship with Him. When you go back, don't make the mistake of not going back far enough. The further you go back, the more you realize you need to go back to God and the relationship you had with Him in the beginning. Some of you have too often gone back to what hurts and you say, "Oh, I remember when I wasn't saved." God wants you to go back further than that. Go back to where your potential started. Go back to the womb.

***Scripture point*: (Isaiah 46:10) Declaring the end from the beginning, and from ancient times things that are not yet done, saying, 'My counsel shall stand, and I will do all My pleasure'.**

God is telling us that what He said He's going to do, He has already done it. We have this idea that God has ordered our steps and tomorrow He's planning a new day for us. No. Our day has been planned before we even showed up. For God said that all things are possible through him ***(Mark 10:27)***.

***Scripture point*: (Genesis 1:1) In the beginning God created the heavens and the earth.**

Before anything was created, God was there. So, as we go back to the beginning, we go back to the former things. We go back to ***Genesis 1:1***, "In the beginning God….."

> ***BULLETIN***: You need to understand that before you embark upon any vision, dream, desire or relationship, you must first bring God in. He must be in the situation before it is formed and while it is still void. Too often people bring God a finished product. The scripture says, "In the beginning, God created…." Let Him create what is without form and what is void in your life.

***Scripture point*: (Genesis 2:2) And on the seventh day God ended His work which He had done, and He rested on the seventh day from all His work which He had done. Then God blessed the seventh day and sanctified it, because in it He rested from all His work which God had created and made**

You are a finished product. God won't come back to do anything else. He's finished. God is finished. Since the beginning, the devil has attempted to convince us that we can do nothing unless God shows up. God is trying to tell us that we can do all things because He has been present since the beginning.

> ***BULLETIN***: Whatever potential you have, you already had it. It's already in you. God is finished.

Because your eyes are focused on the tree, you can't see the whole forest of opportunity ahead of you. God says, no, I have already worked it out. The potential was already in you and complete from the foundation. If God were to have to alter your potential, that makes Him a liar. This idea would imply that God didn't create and birth the potential in you. Fortunately for us, God doesn't lie. The devil is a liar ***(John 8:44)***.

I want to tell you that God created something good from the beginning. If that is so, why are we struggling in places we should already have dominion over? Why do you say, "I know I can do a better job, but they won't give me a chance?" The responsibility isn't on anyone but you. You won't give yourself a chance. You stopped because of what "they" said. You have forgotten the potential you have within yourself. Everything that is birthed in you today was not held up by God until now, but it was given to you when Adam was created. The reason you have not fulfilled all that God has put in you is because you have too much selfishness. You won't stick to the script that God has written for your life and you go off course during the training of your purpose. We remain physically strong but spiritually weak because we won't feed the spirit man what God desired for it to eat. Because of that, we're flesh conscious.

We seek for fast thrills and quick opportunities. The flesh operates in the same manner as a microwave. Let's take a piece of meat as an example. The microwave gives the illusion of fulfilling the same process of cooking the meat as an oven would. When the meat is done in the microwave, it is brown just as it would be in the oven. However, the meat hasn't had a chance to simmer or go through a tenderizing period. When you let microwaved meat sit out, it becomes tasteless really quickly. Well, the spirit man is like an oven. The process takes a lot longer, but it teaches us to be patient and tenderhearted and we begin to develop more flavor because we have gone through a slower process. We are able to endure more pressure and heat that life's obstacles may bring. We need to be patient and allow God to "slow cook" us in the process leading to our purpose. The great thing about God is that He has perfect timing and He will never allow us to be undone or overcooked. God will season you to perfection and prepare you until the appointed time of your potential. You may still be in the preparation process and you can't use your potential now, but it doesn't mean that it is wasted. Only in rushing will you waste potential because what is unused will be thrown away.

***Scripture point*: (Philippians 4:6) Be anxious for nothing, but in everything by prayer and supplication, with thanksgiving, let your requests be made known to God;**

As a child grows up, he says, "I want to be a doctor." Every time he plays outside, he catches insects and dissects them. When his friends come over, he role plays with them, takes their temperatures, and checks their throats. As time goes on, his interest shifts from being a doctor to now becoming a cowboy. Then he goes from wanting to be a cowboy to a major league baseball player. As he enters high school, he begins to put his priorities in order, realizing that he has to have a focal point as it relates to his future in order to be accepted into college. He goes back to his original desire of becoming a doctor and enrolls in biology class. Throughout his adolescence, he tested different areas of interest, but when it came down to it, the original potential of fulfilling a medical career became his heartfelt passion and desire. When he was a young boy, God showed him his potential, but the timing wasn't right. He was still in his season of preparation. Once his process reached the point of opportunity to fulfill his purpose, God opened up the right doors and gave him the wisdom to complete it. The high school student could have said, "I am only a youth and am not qualified to be a doctor", but he trusted the potential that God placed in him ***(Jeremiah 1:7-8)***. Don't let fears conquer your potential.

DON'T QUIT!

2

The Five Principles of Manhood

I want to talk about this thing that makes good people continue along the path of falling into sin. Good people keep missing the mark. It's tired out church doctrine making good, righteous people feel that they can't get deliverance. As a result, they have to walk around with stained lives because they are not free from the thing that God has already freed us from. When I began to search the word of God and his design for man's ultimate potential, I found that God has set a goal that we must look to in order to reach it. In order to step forward and claim our legacy of manhood, womanhood, power, and purpose, we must:

1. Have an intimate interaction with God.
2. Obey God's commandment to work.
3. Cultivate our families.
4. Acknowledge our right to and means of ruling our domain.
5. Attend to the study and understanding of the word of God.

PRINCIPLE 1: Man's intimate interaction with God.

Scripture point: (Genesis 2:8) The Lord God planted a garden eastward in Eden, and there He put the man whom He had formed.

How many really love the Lord with all your heart, but there is suffering going on? Do you know what the suffering is? The suffering is your flesh. It is the flesh standing in the way of your potential. God put the man in the garden of Eden. The garden of Eden signifies the realm of God's presence. The potential of man lies within the presence of God. When God created man, man was in the presence of God. Man did not have to search for an identity. God created man's identity when he created him in His own image. Mankind must recognize this fact. We must get on our knees and constantly acknowledge who God is, and our relationship to Him. What is this suffering that Adam has caused? You may ask the question, "Pastor, how is it possible to suffer, yet have so much joy in God?" There is a war between your flesh and your potential. God has given you a new purpose, but you're living in the old flesh. And it's not that you don't have a desire to do right, but your flesh is so hungry to do wrong because that is all it knows. It's not that you don't want to serve God with all your heart. As a matter of fact, that's all you want to do is serve God with all your heart. Unfortunately, this flesh you have, this old body before you accepted Jesus as your Lord and Savior, this old body that keeps touching things it has no right to touch, begins to crave the evil things in life that are opposed to the things of God. Therefore, we must continually have an intimate interaction with God in order to reach our full potential and not be victims of our flesh. Our flesh isn't the image of God, our spirits are. Our spirits live forever just as God does. The flesh was formed out of the dirt of the ground, but our spirits were created from the breath of God.

PRINCIPLE 2: Man's commandment to work.

***Scripture point*: (Genesis 2:16) And the Lord God commanded the man, saying, "Of every tree of the garden you may freely eat; but of the tree of the knowledge of good and evil you shall not eat, for in the day that you eat of it you shall surely die."**

The thing that really bothers me is that Adam had one commandment, and we have hundreds of them as a result of his negligence in obeying the first command. Adam's one commandment was to work and keep his hands off of one thing! Adam could do anything he wanted.

He could have all the trees, all the animals, and anything else he wanted. He named all the animals. He named all the plants. He named all the things that God created. All Adam had to do was work and refrain from being idle. Idleness leads to sin. God also commanded him what he couldn't do, which was eat from a certain tree. The day you eat of it, you will surely die. Nature will reverse itself. The day he ate the forbidden fruit, everything began to work opposite of its original plan and began to decrease, instead of increase. Everything that lived in Adam's life at this point reversed itself to death. Trees were to have lived forever. All animals were to live forever. He could have prevented all of this by not eating this one thing! Now, take your innocence which keeps life in you and work your potential to its fullest. The moment you do something illegal or immoral, it will cause you to regress, and things will begin to die in your life. Your innocence dies. Your zeal dies. Your joy dies. Your peace dies. All the work you do is in vain. Do the good work in God and obey His commandments.

BULLETIN: Be anxious for nothing and learn not to touch what God has not ordained in your life!

PRINCIPLE 3: Man's command to cultivate.

***Scripture point:* (Genesis 2:15) Then the Lord God took the man and put him in the garden of Eden to tend and keep it.**

Along with God's command to work, the man must know how to cultivate. The man was designed by God to cultivate, build up, strengthen himself and his fellow men and women towards purpose. A cultivating man will encourage, will uphold, will pray that his wife, his child, and his friend will realize their full potential. As a husband, man's whole purpose will be to protect the most valuable part of his wife in the spirit of love, truth, and compassion. The woman is the pillar, and the man the foundation. Men who don't have the principle of cultivation should think twice before actively dating. Take the heat of your passions and refrigerate them. Husbands, if you don't obey the command to cultivate your spouse and children, you will be passing on the legacy of defeat to the generations that follow. God created one man, Adam. He didn't create him to be alone. God chose a helpmate for Adam, which is woman. But, before God gave Adam his helpmate, Adam possessed these principles. Men, you must cultivate, which means cherish her, in order for your union to be complete.

If you love something in the flesh more than you love the woman you're dating, don't get married! You must be complete before covering your wife. You need to cultivate, build, and strengthen. That comes before the desires of your flesh. Get what you need before marriage so that you won't have to suffer while in it.

PRINCIPLE 4: Man's right and means of ruling.

Scripture point: ***(Genesis 2:19) Out of the ground the Lord God formed every beast of the field and every bird of the air, and brought them to Adam to see what he would call them. And whatever Adam called each living creature, that was its name.***

The fourth principle is that man must know how to rule. God never intended on Adam's flesh ruling. It was planned that his spirit would rule. But something happened when Adam disobeyed God's command. The flesh became disobedient. The flesh took the illegal right to govern destiny. That's why you can say, "I'm through with him" in the morning, and knock on his door in the evening.

You can act like you're not going through anything, but I'm telling you something right now, your spirit man is fired up and wants to see the things of God. The reason you don't go to church is because your flesh and your spirit are in a battle. Something is groaning. If you can control your flesh to get out of the bed in the morning, you'll go to church. If you can control your flesh to stop complaining, you'll go and worship God. Nobody sits at home because they want to sit home. It's something about the flesh that makes you not want to come. When you get into the word of God, your flesh wants you to go to sleep, but your spirit says, give me more, give me more.

We've got righteous men of God and anointed women of God, but they still have a flesh problem. God gave Adam authority with his voice to call things out and name them. Men, you are the head of the house, not the slave master. You're the head. The way you talk to your woman will determine what type of person she is. Whether she's a partner or a slave is determined by the way you talk to her and the way you roll your eyes and cut her off. How are you going to cut something off that belongs to you? Unless of course, you picked the wrong rib or the wrong rib picked you. You know you've messed up if she picked you and you had no choice in the matter. Women, you can't be involved with a man that is not fully developed or mature enough to rule his realm. A woman multiplies whatever you give her. So, if her man is jealous, together you will multiply the spirit of jealousy and contempt. If he's sloppy, you will multiply the spirit of confusion. If you give her a house, she'll make it a home. If you give her some groceries, she'll make a meal. If you give her a seed, she'll make a baby. And, if you give her confusion, she'll give you hell. The reason why men are not ruling the way God instructed them to in ***Genesis 2:18*** is because they're not fully walking in His image. Wrong image, wrong ruling. Right image, right ruling.

PRINCIPLE 5: Man's attention to the study and understanding of the word of God.

<u>Scripture point</u>: (Genesis 2:17-18 NKJV) ".....but of the tree of the knowledge of good and evil you shall not eat, for in the day that you eat of it you shall surely die." And the Lord God said, "It is not good that man should be alone;....."

We will be delivered from the bondage and corruption of the flesh by the word of God. Your flesh always wants to tear something down. Isn't it strange that the flesh always wants something that doesn't even belong to it? You can have Willie lying right beside you, still think about Steve, and still want to worship God with all your heart, soul, and mind. Nobody's playing church today. All church players stayed at home. I want some people that say, "I am flesh conscious and I know that this is a problem for me. Sometimes I win, and sometimes I don't, but I don't want to lose any more. I want to be victorious."

Thank God that He's anxiously waiting for you saying, you're going to get here My child, you're going to get here. Study the word, swallow it, and breathe it. Where is here? Here is in the presence, power, and illumination of the word of God, which is able to keep you from falling and find you faultless before His holy presence. In ***Genesis 2:17***, it says that it's not good for man to be alone. It's not talking about any man. It's referring to a man of God who has completed these potentials. What potentials? Well, number one is to always have a desire to be in the presence of God. Secondly, he must have a job that can maintain what he's covering. Number three is that he should know how to encourage, strengthen, and push the woman and children in his life to purpose. Next is that he must be confident enough that he can rule from his heart and not from his fears. And last but certainly not least, he must be a man that speaks the understanding, knowledge and revelation of God to people that are assigned to his life. It is not good for *this* type of man to be alone!

How many of you have awakened with a new feeling of destiny in your life? Something's new. But, you're still struggling with the same flesh. Your spirit gets excited that your flesh wants to do the will of God, and just minutes later, your flesh makes you walk out of it. Then you find yourself trying to fight to come back to God's will. You think you're fighting the obstacles on the outside. You think that this is the problem. That's not the problem, but rather your flesh controlling your mind.

The flesh strives for authority over the mind, and conflicts with the spirit. Oh, you all better hear me because if we can control the flesh, the Spirit will mold us to our full potential. Your spirit man has already lined up with your potential. Your spirit man knows where you're supposed to go. That's why you jump when you hear certain things. That's why a certain scripture can make you go crazy. Because the flesh has history with you, it knows what you like. It knows the figure.

It knows the size. It knows the width. It knows the height. It knows the destiny.

The bible says that we are to walk by faith, and through faith, by the word of God. You have to realize that when you're called to a new destiny, all your flesh knows is what's around you. God is not calling you to what is around you, but He's calling you out of the darkness into the light.

God has prepared a special place for the woman in the life of the five-principled man. Women, if you've got a man with a good job, a nice car, a little money he shares with you every now and then, says sweet things to you, but doesn't have the five principles, he's a malfunctioning man. Beware before you get excited about his Lexus. That's not one of the five principles. Is he tall, dark, and handsome? That again, is not a part of the five principles. Do you have children? If the man in your life does not have these five principles, he could destroy your children. If you're dating a man who doesn't even care to talk to you about your children, he's pathetic. He's not a five-principled man. He's nasty, and in need of a walk with God. A non five-principled man can recognize the loneliness of a woman. He knows the smell of vulnerability. It's in her pores. He smells an opportunity to dominate illegally. They smell the want of attention. He can and will take advantage of it. A woman has a moral obligation to her children, to make sure that any man that comes into her life will carry a commitment to follow these five principles. Your potential and theirs depend upon it.

Men, I have come to tell you, with these five principles working in your lives, you can avoid the contentious woman. With these five principles working in your life, you can bring a woman into your life with whom you can build a relationship of mutual trust and respect. A woman who encourages without nagging, who inspires without harsh words and negative criticism, who gently coaxes, and caresses the five-principled man to unleash his God given potential. It's better to wait for the right rib than to wound or be wounded by so many ribs that could never have a perfect fit. Be patient! Let patience control time. Don't let time control patience.

DON'T QUIT!

3

The Danger of Not Knowing Your Potential

Some of you have gotten stuck, "fat and lazy" stuck, just sitting around talking about what you wish you could do. "I could if I had a chance." So why don't you have a chance? The truth is, you had the same chance I've had. In six years, I was pastoring a church of several hundred, but only started with sixteen people. I'm no better than the next person. I'm just not intimidated about my potential. Learn to stay focused in the lane that God called you to, so that jealousy won't rise up and cause an accident. Success can stop your potential. You may not believe this, but success can be a danger to your potential, and, once achieved, it can bring it to a halt. Why? Because you begin to think you have already arrived and you don't have to struggle anymore. You then begin to lose the drive to extend your potential. "Look at the trophies I have", you'll say. Isn't that typical of many of the so-called successful people of today? They build their fortune and now they're useless. They fail to realize that success is not enough, and they've got more in them. Don't get so comfortable that comfort kills potential in you.

I remember when I first started pastoring my church and the number of people God started to bless me with in a short period of time. I would be around seasoned pastors and would start telling them of my concerns, one of which was that I was only bringing in a third of my congregation on Wednesday nights. When I told them that, they said, "A congregation your size and you're getting a third? Man with my congregation, I can't even get a tenth of the people to come out on a weekday service. You've got it going on. You have it together." If I had listened to that, I would have stayed with a third. It would have stopped the potential in me and I would have been dying with the praise of people. I regrouped and began to rethink things, remembering that they didn't create me, and, with God my success was limitless. I couldn't stop for celebration, or pause for praise. It's not time for my celebration until I complete God's will. What God assigned me to is different than what He assigned you to. Although we end up at the same finish line, we all have different processes to get there. Trust in the Lord with all your heart and lean not to your own understanding ***(Proverbs 3:5)***. What's your understanding? What people show you and tell you. In all your ways acknowledge Him. To acknowledge Him is to reverence a supreme being who has a further outlook and purpose in your vision. Through acknowledging God, He shall direct every step and path of your life. A path is your process that leads to the road of your potential. No process, no purpose.

Let's expose some of the dangers in not knowing your potential:

1. If you don't know your potential, you will damage other people's potential.
2. If you don't know your potential, other people will prostitute your potential.
3. If you don't know your potential, you will die with wasted potential.

BULLETIN: Jealousy will destroy your potential.

When you don't know your potential, the devil will use the spirit of jealousy, because jealousy allows God to leave the presence of your potential.

Scripture point: ***(Ezekiel 8:5-6) Then He said to me, "Son of man, lift your eyes now toward the north". So I lifted my eyes toward the north, and there, north of the altar gate, was this image of jealousy in the entrance. Furthermore He said to me,***

"Son of man, do you see what they are doing, the great abominations that the house of Israel commits here to make Me go far away from My sanctuary?....."

Jealousy allows you to fight for a position that you should release. This is a spirit that you don't use on yourself, but others. Most jealous people become insecure when they see someone that has the image of fulfilling something they think they should have. Before he was satan, Lucifer was a worshipper in God's house, but became jealous of the praise that God was given. He coveted a position that he was not assigned to. Satan thought he was greater than God, so he permitted jealousy to alter his potential and purpose in God. He looked toward the wrong direction, therefore putting himself out of his place. I am emphasizing jealousy because it has great power to blind your ability to see your potential.

BULLETIN: When you don't know your potential, you will allow the enemy to fill void spaces in your life. The ultimate danger of not knowing your potential is that God created something He cannot use.

In not knowing your potential, something that may be great will die because it was never discovered. You can never judge a person's abilities that you see to determine their potential. I know a millionaire who knew, and acted on his potential. According to society, he should be a poor, dependant man, who would never obtain anything because of his inability to "function" suitably. This man had a third or fourth grade education. Several people have asked the question, "Since he was so limited in his education, then how did he become a millionaire?" The answer is simple. He is a millionaire because he knew what God had called him to be. He didn't feel sorry for himself because of his deficiencies. He had challenges, but he was so determined to fulfill God's plan for his life, that he didn't let intimidation set in because of his flaws. Don't let your flaws interfere with knowing your purpose.

BULLETIN: Wrong slogans bring wrong power.

Every person has flaws. Just don't let your flaws have you. There was a group that flew from one city to another to minister. The climate and change in the environment affected the singers' vocal cords. As they began to minister, the power of God moved in the service. While singing, the change in their vocal cords made the higher octaves hard to reach. Not recognizing that the power of God had already moved through them, one of the lead singers said, "The devil got our voices, but that's alright. We're going to praise God anyway!" I jokingly whispered to one of my ministers saying, "If the devil has her voice, we shouldn't believe anything she says!" Of course, I was being sarcastic, but she never should have let that shortcoming override her potential. The work was already done, even with her inadequacy to fulfill what she knew she had the ability to do. We can't give credit to flaws. That only strengthens the work of the adversary. Where man is limited, God isn't.

DON'T QUIT!

4

Whatever God Planned For You To Be, You Can Be

<u>Scripture point</u>: (Hebrews 11:1) Now faith is the substance of things hoped for, the evidence of things not seen.

This just in: Faith is not something that began with the teaching of Christ in the New Testament. It existed from the beginning, when God created all living things and said that it was good. Whatever God planned for you to be, you can be. Your destiny was already written by the word of God. It is up to you to find and declare what that destiny is through faith and prayer.

<u>Scripture point</u>: (Hebrews 11:3) By faith we understand that the worlds were framed by the word of God so that things which are seen were not made of things which are visible.

So, the question is, is your destiny already written by the word of God? Consider this — whatever God ordained you to do, He already created the provisions for you to do it. It's already there. Why are you whining? If He told you to do it and you're in line with faith, then guess what? Whatever you need to make happen, is already there. Why worry about temporal affairs, such as, how a person feels or thinks about you. "Why am I tall or short? I won't fit in because I am from another culture, and another city. I don't have a degree." Why do we get so worried about those things? If it's in line with God, it can only work for the better ***(Romans 8:28).*** That scripture declares that you have no right to panic! We must always be mindful that our situations are not our gods, and not even the devil can stop your destiny when it's in line with God. The only one that stops your destiny when it's in line with God is you! Like it or not, you have been mad at the wrong person. Say to yourself, "Step aside satan, I'm the problem!" You've been judging the wrong thing. That's why you can't go forward, because you're not in line. In line with what? With the will of, and faith in God. We give satan too much credit. In your life, satan may have bothered or attacked you ten times. The rest of your issues came from decisions you've made. No faith, no vision. No vision, no journey. No journey, no purpose. No purpose, no existence. So, faith is for the journey of your purpose, not just for the journey. You don't need faith to get a house. You need good credit. You don't need faith to keep your job. You need to be a good employee. You don't need faith to lose weight. You need to eat less and exercise more. Keep in mind that the devil is not attacking you, but you are attacking yourself by misusing your faith.

Let's begin to use our faith in the proper order to receive all that God has planned for our purpose. So, why is faith necessary? It is needed for the oppositions of your process to keep you from walking away from, fighting against, or talking negatively about it. That's when scripture should rise up from your belly to declare that, "I can do *all* things through Christ which strengthens me" ***(Philippians 4:13)***. You are being attacked by the visual and have not entered the spiritual. That's when you need to be assured that, "No weapon that is formed against you shall prosper" ***(Isaiah 54:17)***. Why should you affirm these things? Because He is in me and I am in Him. "Greater is He who is in me than he who is in the world" ***(1 John 4:4)***!

Scripture points: ***(Philippians 1:6) ....being confident of this very thing, that He who has begun a good work in you will complete it until the day of Christ Jesus.***

(Jeremiah 1:5) "Before I formed you in the womb I knew you; before you were born I sanctified you; I ordained you a prophet to the nations."

(Matthew19:26) But Jesus looked at them and said to them, "With man this is impossible, but with God all things are possible."

Some circumstances may seem to be stopping your process, but it's actually molding the potential God needs in you to become the leader, ambassador, or disciple He called you to be in this season leading into your purpose.

> ***BULLETIN:*** Spend more time praising God, and less time complaining about the devil.

Scripture points: ***(James 1:2-3) My brethren, count it all joy when you fall into various trials, knowing that the testing of your faith produces patience.***

(Psalm 30:5) For His anger is but for a moment, His favor is for life; Weeping may endure for a night, but joy comes in the morning.

DON'T QUIT!

5

The Importance of Growing In The Spirit

Another roadblock to realizing your full potential is becoming comfortable and lazy, relaxed into the common places of life. God desires more from you if you've been doing the normal dancing and praising year in and year out. These are not the only things that God wants out of your potential. These things are signs of victory or encouragement, but the spirit man is designed to lead and direct you to your fullest potential. There is a price you pay to keep it fresh and alive, and that is totally trusting the Holy Spirit in all directions of your life. His purpose is not to go against you, but to show you the way to attain the greatest level of potential within you. We must establish daily communication with the Holy Spirit. We need to allow the Holy Spirit to have full reign in our lives, making it possible for Him to lead us. Under His direction, we are directly connected to all that God has ordained us to become. To be connected to the Holy Spirit allows us to be connected to Jesus, and to be connected to Jesus allows us to be connected to God. Without the leading of the Holy Spirit, there is no positive direction.

If you did the same thing last year, and you can only remember doing the same thing the year before, you are not totally pleasing God. You are in a rut, deactivating the potential within you. Do you think God loves your praise if all you're doing is the same thing you did last year, sitting in the same seat, looking at the same people? Do you think God accepts that as being the best that you can do? Do *you* honestly think that this is the best you can do? That is only the best that you can do without the Holy Spirit. Can you recall every New Year's Eve that you jump up and down praising the Lord that He let you make it over, but yet you can't search the whole congregation and find one person you led to Christ in the entire year? That's wasting the potential God gave you to use for others. Every New Year's Eve service, you should be able to search the congregation and see what your testimony has led to Christ. If not, you are celebrating in vain because it's not only what God has done for you which makes the service powerful, but also what you have done for Him. Then you can celebrate!

You can't grow if you don't exercise your full potential. Being nice is good, but it is not enough. I don't care how nice you are. Not exercising your creativity to expand your potential is not going to do the trick. God didn't say, "Be nice and you'll please Me." It has nothing to do with being nice. Many Christians believe being saved is enough. God desires discipleship. The Holy Spirit will lead you to people who need what you have, and direct you to people who have what you need. That is the beginning stage of discipleship. Helping one another towards Christ.

Have you been called to preach? You have great potential, but have you acted on it? Have you studied to show yourself approved ***(2 Timothy 2:15)***? If you study to show yourself approved, you won't have to use spiritual excuses such as, "Praise the Lord, I really wasn't prepared for you to call on me, but, God is good!" Those words prohibit the Holy Spirit from fulfilling all that you are, in your potential. If you would rely on Him, He will bring all things that you've studied back to your remembrance. Exercise your anointing. Expand your mind, and your horizons will expand with it. Otherwise, you will not please God. You must strive to be effective.

The Holy Spirit changes your nature so that the old man doesn't have power over the new vision in your life. Are you introverted? Become extroverted. Just talking won't do it. You may say, "It's not my personality." Then change your personality and walk in faith. When you're in Christ, you're a new creature. Old things have passed away ***(2 Corinthians 5:17)***. That means, when you realize your potential, your personality changes. Your nature changes. All of a sudden, you start doing things to show forth your love and appreciation for what God has put within you. The potential is already in you. You must recognize and confirm that the joy of the Lord is your strength ***(Nehemiah 8:10)***. Joy is an outward emotion that expresses an inward feeling. Christians should be the happiest, most zealous, talkative people in the world. For we have the good news. So, it's not about your personality, it's about God's purpose shining through you. Remember that the Holy Spirit is here as a comforter and guide, and He develops you into all that you are called to be.

Scripture point: (Hebrews 11:6).....for he who comes to God must believe that He is, and that He is a rewarder of those who diligently seek Him.

In order to grow in the spirit, you first and lastly must seek God. Get excited about your destiny in God. Get excited about the seed that God has planted in you that you haven't built up yet. There are books that have not yet been written because you don't think you have the seed to do it. There are songs that have not been recorded yet. There are cures that have not been discovered yet. AIDS has no business destroying the earth, but somebody that has the cure refuses to birth the potential in them. Learn to encourage yourself. Do you remember how David in the bible had things taken from him, like friends and family? People stopped believing in him. However, he began to encourage himself. He began to prepare himself to worship. I learned that when it gets hard for me and people don't believe I have the potential, I will prepare a party for myself. The party I prepare is not a pity party, but a praise and worship party. I begin to awaken newness of potential. One scripture to stand on in times of being discouraged is ***1 John 4:4***. This scripture declares that I can tap into my full level of potential, as long as I am connected to the right source. There will be seasons where people will encourage you to go. Normally, people will encourage you when they see it, but you have to learn to encourage yourself when they don't.

DON'T QUIT!

6

The Tree of Life

<u>Scripture point</u>: (John 15:5) "I am the vine, you are the branches. He who abides in Me, and I in him, bears much fruit; for without Me, you can do nothing."

We have been talking about potential as it relates to dominion over God's creation. But, the moment you get to where you think you're a King Midas or Queen Cleopatra, and cancel God out, you diminish your potential. You cut yourself off from the source. As the scripture point puts it, you cut yourself off from the vine. When you think more highly of yourself than you ought, and think that you cannot be touched, or, your pride is a mountain that no one can climb, you will begin to have thoughts such as, "Nobody can tell me what to do", or "Nobody is going to talk to me that way." This attitude indicates that you can do things by yourself, and you don't need God. But, God's word tells us that if we want to be successful, then we've got to be connected to the everlasting vine. God says, "I am the vine" ***(John 15:5)***. And with all authority, He attaches you to Himself. You are now God's connection. You are the branches that come out of Him.

Now, the vine and the tree are alike as fruit-bearers. The substance of the tree is in its branches. If we then, are the branches of the tree, why don't we have the power of God? The glory of the branches is the fruit that they bear. But, we have borne strange fruit. Why else are we broken, busted and disgusted? Is this the fruit of the vine? God forbid. But, when we fail to fulfill our potential, that's what we have come to. We've been cut off the tree and become useless, like all the other branches lying on the ground. We're dead, dry, and brittle, still thinking we still can be used because people are picking us up and swinging us. You're being used alright, but not to the glory of God. You weren't created as a useless stick, you were created to rule. You were created to stretch out and see things grow in yourself, and see things multiply. Instead, we've become a mound of broken branches, standing on the corner, wasting potential, joining the other broken branches, sitting on similar corners. I see a girl who is a broken branch, looking for a man that is a broken branch. They join together and become stagnate. Nothing comes of their union, and nothing grows from it. No God in them because they are unripe fruit, failing to develop into maturity. So much wasted potential.

Ever eat fruit that wasn't ripe? Ever get hold of a banana that's not ripe? Go and get one of those plums that's hard and sour, falling off the tree. You'll see what I mean. Make sure your fruit is nice, juicy and ripe, so that when it does fall from the tree, it can multiply and realize its full potential. Remember, in the eye of God, an apple is not just an apple, it is an orchard, turning into a forest of apple orchards, which are hundreds of trees, but from one apple. In being a branch, beware that you don't grow into so much pride that you are disconnected from the vine, not depending on the vine's source for survival. Sometimes, when we begin to accomplish so many things, and leaves are flourishing in our lives, we forget we're only an extension to the real source. If we cut the source off, eventually every green thing attached to you will die. Cut off God, cut off life. Stay connected to God, stay connected to eternal life ***(John 15:5)***.

You may see yourselves as one piece of fruit, but in reality, you have the potential to become a forest. God created you, and when He created you, He had the idea of a forest in mind. In life, there are many family trees that start with a mother. Then, it goes from the mother to the daughter, from the daughter to her son, and from the son to his children. The way you view a family tree is seeing each person individually. Their potential is unbounded. The mother is a nurse, whose daughter is a cosmetologist, whose son goes to college. While, another works at social security, and another owns a local business. We don't realize that what we take as a single personality, in reality, is a stalk from the tree, and was inside the belly of the mother. Eyes have not seen, and ears have not heard what God has prepared for you ***(1 Corinthians 2:9)***. You're struggling for no reason. Your mind has to change. You're going out there trying to fight for a career, trying to fight to get an identity. God says, no, it's already in the bag. It's already prepared. You must know who and what you are in order to realize your full potential. The potential that allows you to be all that God intended for you to be is already inside of you. We have too much potential to be living without hope. Too much potential.

Stop being limited in your thinking. Stop looking at your surroundings through the small end of the scope. There is a house that's not built yet, not even designed, and no one has even thought of the structure of this home, yet it's already prepared for you. Eyes have not seen. God has already prepared it.

There is a healing of all diseases coming out of one person's hand because God already prepared it, but you don't think it because no one has ever done it. You say, "It can't be done. It's impossible." No! It's not impossible ***(Matthew 17:20)***. You think it is impossible because that is all *you* think you can do. But, you must expand your mind, challenge the darkness, and shed light where you can.

Study to make yourself acceptable and useful. It doesn't matter if you were conceived in a station wagon. Your potential is as broad and varied as anyone else's. Remember, Christ was born in a stable. It was already prepared. It doesn't matter if it was at a five star hotel or a cheap inn. It was already prepared. It doesn't matter if somebody threw you away on the wayside. It was already prepared. God knows the mess from which you come and the path to lead you out. Yes, He has prepared it. You have to understand that the only reason God prepared it is because He wants you to fulfill your potential in Him. God is always preparing a way of escape for those He loves. As long as your mess is not greater than your purpose, you can always grow out of it. But, when your mess becomes greater than your purpose, it can lose its value. Only God can determine that. Don't let your failure determine your end. Just say, "I must be called to great things because God is not through with me yet."

DON'T QUIT!

7

Awaken Your Brain, Awaken Your Full Potential

Some college graduates can't remember what they learned two years after college. That's how man has trained you. He has trained you to go through the process, but not learn anything. It is said that we only use ten percent of our brain's potential. It is also said that the brain is unique. How can something that's only being used ten percent of the time be unique? More unique than the brain, is how we can use our faith. You are ill, and the doctor says it's incurable. Looks like you're going to die. You pray to God to activate your healing power. All of a sudden, during your next doctor's visit, he says, "I don't know what's going on, but what looked incurable is now not there at all." How did that work? It worked because you used faith. It's okay to pray that God would increase your level of faith and belief. In ***Mark 9:24***, a distressed father comes to Jesus in tears for the healing of his son. He tells Jesus, "Lord I believe, but help my unbelief."

What is faith? Utilizing that which you never knew you had. Activating that part of the brain to tell your body to behave! You say, "That's not what I am or where I'm going." You have your healing from faith, which God has already placed within you. Where is it housed? It is housed in the part of your brain that you don't use. What part of the brain do we use then? We use the survival part. That's all we have been doing, is trying to survive. So, we use the part of the brain that gets us over. This is the part of the brain that talks junk and ignores the strategies to get around obstacles. God has ordained that, through faith, mountains will move ***(Matthew 17:20)***. Pray to God that your faith may increase. Pray that it may trigger an awakening in that part of the brain to use the other ninety percent. When you have expanded your awareness to the point of its potential, take the time to nurture it. What stops us from taking time to nurture it? Pride. Yes, pride will block your potential.

Scripture point: ***(Proverbs 6:16) These six things the Lord hates, yes, seven are an abomination to Him: A proud look, . . .***

Pride will raise a wall between you and your potential. If you want to awaken the potential in yourself, you have to relinquish the pride that shackles your potential. Take a child that does not submit to his parent. That child will poke his lip out, swell his chest up, roll his eyes at you, and want to fight with you. That is a mannish child that is heading for what? A stern correction. But, a child that is submissive, a child that can accept correction, is a child that will go somewhere. That is a child that will fulfill his or her potential.

Having imagination and talent is not enough. Look at all the talented and imaginative people you know and ask yourselves where they are. The spirit of pride has destroyed potential. Being proud will always produce offspring and one of the offspring produced from being proud is a lie. Some lie with complete comfort. But, God hates it. "Oh I only told a little lie." But, God hates it. He hates it because it's not what He created you to have dominion over. When you lie, you're intimidated and afraid of life's consequences. You're afraid to move ahead to a higher level of existence. You are afraid to explore and expand your potential.

Our offspring, our children, are dying. Whatever our potential, our greatest fruit is our children. Mothers and fathers need to always be in prayer for their children. They need to be stretched out in supplication, not on the phone talking about, "I don't know what's wrong with that girl", or, "I don't know what to do about that boy." Our steps are ordered by God, who loves you. If we are to work toward the highest potential for our children, we must bury our faces in that pillow, and kneel to our knees, saying, "That's my son or daughter Lord. You didn't design them like that. You gave them to me, God, and now I'm giving them back to You to fix it."

God is passionate that we should get it right and stop using only ten percent of our brain. We fail to maintain the power we were given in Genesis, and we take on the curse that cuts our power off because of this. God says we are the body of Christ. Every day, we are destroying the potential of one another. In the coming week, try not to be jealous. Try to love people and work together positively. Call people and say, "Hello, God loves you." Go visit the sick. Expand yourself and God will bless you. Try it for a week, then rest. I'm not saying that you won't have any discord, no arguments, no confusion, no lying, but, in this week, you're going to find some lovely things to say, like, "Wow, he's home and I'm glad."

Let God expand your brain beyond the ten percent. Instead of having that back seat mentality of just doing things enough to get over, start saying, "Now, let me plan to multiply." The fruit ought to end up being a branch. The whole purpose of potential is to become fruitful. After all the shouting, dancing, and rolling is done, you are only tired. After all the hysterics, there is no knowledge. And, if we're not careful, we will jump up and down, but not possess any power. What power comes with that? Train yourself to jump up when you've created something. When you see your house built from the ground up, then you should jump up and give the glory to God. Create something when you see your family falling apart, and by the power of the Holy Ghost, you can step in and bring all things together. When you see people who have sicknesses and diseases, having all types of addictions, and you activate that Holy Ghost brain power, that's when you jump. It's the Holy Ghost that comes in and activates the brain. You must have the Holy Ghost. Jesus says, "I must go but I will leave you a Helper. He will guide you into all truth" ***(John 16:13)***. All means *All*! The word of God says, "The truth shall make you free" ***(John 8:32)***. Our power comes through our partnership with the Holy Spirit. ***DON'T QUIT!***

8

Making The Wrong Right

<u>Scripture point</u>: (Proverbs 6:16) These six things the Lord hates, yes seven are an abomination to Him: A proud look, a lying tongue, hands that shed innocent blood, a heart that devises wicked plans, feet that are swift in running to evil, a false witness who speaks lies, and one who sows discord among the brethren.

All of those things are roadblocks to potential. Did you notice that of the things God says He hates, not one deals with sex outside of the marriage relationship? Don't misunderstand me, it's wrong, but people have strayed away from what is abominable in the sight of the Lord, forgetting that they will be judged for lying, pride of spirit, deceitfulness, talking about people, tearing people's names down, and blood on their hands for destroying people's lives and potential. Now, let's focus on the false witness who speaks lies.

I have come across hustlers that were selling—they weren't selling in the church, but they were selling on the street. They came to me as hustlers, because that's all they knew. But, they were honest. They didn't try to fake it, like everything was fine, hoping no one would notice.

"You're high, brother." "I'm not high, I always look like this. I'm no junky, and I'm not doing drugs." "Your skin is reeking alcohol." "Look, I haven't been drinking." "Well then, you better stop sweating like you have." "Man, you know I always sweat." "Yeah, but your sweat doesn't have to smell like that!"

You know, the usual cat and mouse. No. These hustlers came to me and said, Pastor, this is my predicament. I want out. I'm trapped. They didn't lie to the man of God. They were honest with me. They came to me and told me their concerns. Most pastors would have turned their backs on these folks. They would have told them they were wrong for doing that.

The point is, I was worried about their souls, and I knew their souls couldn't be saved if they were in a trapped position. I didn't play with them. I went to God. I prayed about their predicament, and told God that they would need a way of escape. When dealing with your full potential, you've got to lay your cards on the table with God, approach Him boldly with no minced words. "God, show me the way of my escape." Make it personal. Then I asked God this question, "God, how much time do they have to work this out?" God gave me two answers. He gave me how much time they had, and told me the people in their lives that they had to deal with, in order to escape from harm.

I went to them and said, "Leave this person alone", and "You have this much time." The person I told them to leave alone eventually landed in jail. The attachment would have landed them there also. They cleaned up their lives, obeyed the law, severed their attachments, and, in time, got on the road to fulfilling their full potential.

God's purpose is to get the full potential out of you, even it if means severing ties, and making sure there is no evidence on you. God desires you to experience your full potential. You can't let it be done through selfish ambition. You can't lie to people. Why? Because, it blocks your potential. Once you create a lie, you have to live with it.

This just in: There is a war between the passions of the mind and the desire for spiritual things that is destroying your potential. How many of you all have awakened, and God has given you a new feeling of destiny in your life? Something's new. But you're still struggling with that same mind-set, which is the desire to please the body. God has given you a desire to realize your potential, but because you're still striving to satisfy the passions of your mind, you don't have a desire to do it. It's not that you don't want to serve God with all your heart. As a matter of fact, that's all you want to do is serve God with your whole heart, but, the mind-set that you had before you accepted Jesus as your personal savior keeps hungering for the evil things of life. This mind-set will continue to drive you away from your potential. We have too many righteous men and women that still have a desire to please the passions that are controlling their minds and are steadily destroying their potential. Oh, you all better hear me. Overcome your passions and let loose your potential!

In dealing with potential, we must understand that the earth is the Lord's and the fullness thereof and they that dwell within ***(1 Corinthians 10:26).*** Simply speaking, everything on the earth belongs to God, from the cattle, to the grass, to the trees. Everything on earth. From the stars and the moon, to the sky. Everything belongs to God. There is nothing we have that belongs to us. Our full potential comes from God, but our failures come from us. We're the only ones that can stop ourselves from achieving what God has ordained. God has ordained that we have dominion over the earth.

***Scripture point:* (Genesis 1:28) Then God blessed them, and God said to them, "Be fruitful and multiply; fill the earth and subdue it; have dominion over the fish of the sea, over the birds of the air, and over every living thing that moves on the earth."**

God turned control over to us. He gave us the power to rule our potential as our own. Whatever becomes of the creation, is left to the humans He has created. The potential of all rests with the man. Issues such as air pollution and famine, God is saying, are in our hands. We are short changed because we think too small. As a result, man has become duped and confused by the devil. God gave us dominion over all His creation, yet we turn around and do what? Drown in a sea of troubles because we can't handle it.

Why do we beg, beseech, and request God to give us that which we already have to fulfill our potential? We've become the most excuse making, complaining and perpetrating, phony, everybody-out-for-themselves type of people, and have lost the fundamental concept that we are made in the image of God. Thus, we have not developed ourselves spiritually to possess that which is our due, our full potential, which is our purpose.

To realize full potential, we must grow in spirit as well as in flesh. We were never designed to lean on another man's dream when we can dream ourselves. We were created to fulfill our potential, which is to have dominion over the earth. The reason why we don't have dominion is because we really don't know who we are, so we don't know what we have to rule over. Because of this, we've become imitators, copying and creating something that we were not called to do. One thing we were called to do is cultivate and direct people, not to intimidate or destroy them. In ***Ezekiel 8:3-6***, it talks about how God began to reveal to man what stands between Him and you, which is jealousy. It stands at the front and the back of so many illegal destinies. He says, "Son of man, do you see what they are doing, to make Me go far away from My sanctuary?" Jealousy closes the door to the voice of God. No voice, no direction. No direction, no purpose. No purpose, no existence. Don't let jealousy rule you.

DON'T QUIT!

9

Watch The Tares

<u>Scripture point</u>: (Matthew 13:26) But when the grain had sprouted and produced a crop, then the tares also appeared, so the servants of the owner came and said to him, sir, did you not sow good seed in your field? How then does it have tares?

I have found in my life, especially in my ministry, my potential tested—potentially stopped by those in my own congregation, and those whom I'd considered friends and loyal supporters. They began questioning my very foundation as a man and as a pastor. "Pastor Tony", they'd say, "I thought you were building a good church? I thought things were happening in your ministry? I thought you had it going on? How is it that you've got converts back out on the corner? How is it that you've got some ex-thug crying and whining when he finds himself in trouble and a jail sentence hanging over his head, rolling around the altar saying, Jesus, Jesus, and as soon as his prayers are answered, and he's off the hook, all of a sudden, he's lying , denying and conniving, falling back into his own vomit?" He might be down, but not for the count. With God's help, he's going to pull out and realize his potential. With faith in the amazing grace of God, I'm going to say, "Wait, hold on, you're going to get there. You're going to make it. You might fall a couple of times, but you're going to get there. You're going to groan, but you're going to get there." I've come to let you know, it doesn't matter what you've done, you're going to get there. It doesn't matter what you're going through, you're going to get there, because God is anxiously waiting for you to realize your potential. He's waiting. He has not left. He's still waiting.

You must stay focused and do what you were created to do. There will always be enemies when you start expanding your potential. When the membership in our church began exploding, when our outreach in the community began to change lives, the tares arose in the form of slander saying that, "Brother so-and-so had 20 men out there selling his drugs, and sister this-and-that was out hustling and selling her body." The tares were attacking not the pastor, but the membership. Nothing good ever comes from the tares. A woman thirty years removed from the street life is driven out of the church or off her job by a rumor of long ago. Dead truth. Nothing but the tares trying to destroy potential. An ex-drug addict walks into the house at a family reunion and is still seen as a crack head. Been clean for ten years, has a job, three kids, and a mortgage, but destroyed by vicious, back-stabbing tares. Don't let the tares of the past become the weeds of the present that slow down and destroy your future. Their whole purpose is to tear at your potential. The only thing that needs to remind you of your ugliness is the thing that saved you from it, and that is the cross. Be careful to always remember that the seed is planted by people who want to support your potential. The tare is planted by people who want to choke out the potential in you. Both of them are planted in the infant stages of your life. Some tares will grow for years, just to attack you one time and choke the life out of your purpose. But remember to be steadfast, immovable, always abounding in the work of the Lord, knowing that your labor is not in vain in the Lord ***(1 Corinthians 15:58)***.

The invasion of the tares:

To be invaded by the tares is a frightful thing. The weak and the frightened who can't bear to face the music of their own actions or interactions, are suddenly reduced to being judges of others' actions and potential. They see the ripeness of your fields and the potential of your crop and begin to kill your harvest, mess up your reputation, destroy your vision. They become the weeds of negativity and begin to strangle the positive. We're concerned about our crop. We want to make sure that when we pull the weeds out, that the good does not get tangled with it. We don't want to push anyone out of their purpose. I am called to cultivate you because God called me to be a farmer over his crop. Because you don't like what's going on in the church, we can't pluck out the tares indiscriminately. If you pluck them out before their time, you may do irreparable harm. If you pluck one member out, it will affect another. When we are full grown in the word attached to Christ, being wrapped around with weeds doesn't mean it is not a good plant.

There are times when we're seeking God for our true purpose and potential, that we find ourselves among the tares, in negative environments or amongst negative people, that try to keep us from reaching our full potential. What we have to realize is that God uses our trials and challenges to pull out the best in us, so rather than allowing the tares to distract or destroy us, we should let them build us and push us to our purpose. The bible teaches us to "…..count it all joy when you fall into various trials……because the trying of our faith produces patience…..that we may be perfect and complete, lacking nothing" ***(James 1:2-4)***. In other words, the path to perfection and potential is through our trials, negative circumstances, and our tares.

DON'T QUIT!

> ***BULLETIN:*** A man assumes who he is by what he thinks, but knows who he is by what he goes through.

A man or woman in search of their potential will turn negative situations into positive inspiration. Think of a child growing up in an environment of substance abuse, poverty, and little to no opportunity for education. He's surrounded by tares. As that child matures into adulthood, he must decide whether he'll be a victim of his environment or if he'll use it as inspiration to have a better life and to live out his full potential.

BULLETIN: A man without a purpose will allow his environment to pull him down. A man with a purpose will allow his environment to push him up.

The problem is, we choose to keep the tares from our past, bring them into our present, and allow them to influence our future. Why is it that we can't let go of the tares, even when it's affecting our harvest? I was counseling a young woman who God has blessed with a wonderful husband and family, but she refused to let go of the tares. She was holding on to past relationships with all of the pain and drama, and it was destroying her harvest. Her marriage was falling apart, her children were being neglected and her integrity as a woman of God was compromised. All of this resulted from her decision to hold on to the tares.

You see, Jesus tells us in ***Matthew 13:24-30*** and ***Matthew 13:36-43,*** that we will have seasons in our life where the tares are growing right along with the wheat. When the time for harvest comes, the tares would be bound together and destroyed, meaning they would no longer be able to affect our destiny, unless of course, we choose to keep them around. The tares must be burned in order to destroy the seed, because they will otherwise continue to grow and affect who God is calling you to be.

10

Your Potential Is God's Harvest

Your potential is God's harvest. The whole purpose of realizing your potential is to become fruitful. Some are exceptional writers of poetry. Some are incredible painters and musicians. Whatever fruit your talent produces, take courage to bring it forth and give the glory to God. Create something unique with your God-given potential, through the power of the Holy Ghost. Activate that Holy Ghost brain power with prayer power, for eyes have not seen and ears have not heard the good that will emerge when you've unleashed your full potential ***(1 Corinthians 15:58)***. As a child, Moses had the potential to travel through a river, and as a man to lead people out of the hands of Pharaoh. As a child, David had the potential to handle bears and lions, and to protect sheep, but also had the potential to slay a giant to protect the people. Daniel had the potential to serve the king, but not above his God. Shadrach, Meshach, and Abednego all had the potential not to bow down to the king who threatened them, but to bow down to God who protected them. Mary Magdalene had the faith to be delivered from demonic spirits and also had the potential to talk to Jesus after His death and resurrection. Your potential is not who you are today, that's your success, but your potential is who you're going to become in the future.

We need to give God the fullness of our potential and not just the sprouts in the beginning stage of growth. Most people give God a small plant, but expect a large harvest in return. Let me give you an example. You can put an apple in your hand. The apple has potential to be used for various purposes such as apple juice, applesauce, apple pie, and apple butter. It doesn't end there. An apple has the potential to grow into a tree, which then turns into a forest. However, if the potential of the apple is never utilized to the fullest, the apple will eventually begin to spoil, and the potential it had is now wasted. To give God the fullness of your potential, you need to find out how to produce the most out of who you are.

The example of the apple gives you the potential of the fruit, but it doesn't mention the process. The harvest that comes from the apple is the apple juice, applesauce, apple pie, and apple butter. But, the process of the harvest is cutting into the apple, finding the seed, planting the seed in good ground, waiting for the trees to spring up, and waiting for the season of ripeness. Once you follow the process, then the apple's potential can be used in its fullness to produce the harvest. In giving God the fullness of your potential, you must be willing to lose something in order to gain something. You have to allow something or someone to cut into you in order to develop you. As you cut into the apple, it's not the skin or the fruit of the apple, but it's the seed of the apple that has the ability to produce a large harvest. Every great potential has a seed. God sent Jesus on the earth as a seed so He could plant the disciples. As a result, the disciples planted many sons and daughters in the gospel to produce God's harvest.

I'm going to give you three scenarios of planting seed to receive God's harvest:

Scenario 1: In ministry, there are pastors who've founded churches, and established a congregation of thousands. The pastor developed sons in the gospel out of the congregation. In order for the seed within the potential of that pastor to grow into a forest, that pastor must release his sons in the gospel with people who will support their ministry. The people he sends out with the sons in the gospel will represent the soil that supports the foundation of the potential, which will become a great forest of leaders. In following this process, the vision of the pastor will not die when he or she dies. If the ministry is built around that pastor and is not shared, when the season of the pastor is over, and seed has not been planted into other leaders of the congregation, the closure of the pastor will also be the closure of the seed. I must remind you, that as you begin to sow seed into your leaders, your leaders will establish an identity. Don't allow this transition to result in anger, jealousy, or frustration. It will harden the ground of the potential of the seed. Your potential is God's harvest. We're trying to build a forest instead of holding on to a piece of fruit.

Scenario 2: Releasing your potential into others will make it greater. Some businesses are established by people who carried out the potential of an ancestor. There was a restaurant owner whose great grandmother had a delicious recipe for macaroni and cheese. Great grandma never measured the ingredients, but used a pinch of this and a handful of that. Great grandma taught her daughter how to make the macaroni and cheese, and her daughter paid attention and wrote the recipe down. The daughter had a little girl and as the little girl got older, she shared the recipe with her. Well, the young woman got smart and wanted to make some money off of this original recipe, so she had it published in a cookbook. This woman ended up having a son. She taught him how to cook because she felt it was necessary for him to be independent. As the son got older, he loved to cook so much that he opened up his own restaurant. One of the specialty menu items was called "Grandma's down home mac-n-cheese". Everyone who ordered this menu item loved it. This is an example of a process that started with a seed and turned into a forest. You can't be intimidated or selfish because you don't want to allow other people to strengthen the potential. Keep in mind that your potential is God's harvest.

Scenario 3: One way that a seed can turn into a forest is through our personal evangelism. There was a man that God instructed to do a five day revival. He spoke to the man and said that if he did this revival, then thousands would be saved. The man got excited and prepared for the revival. He went out and got a tent and bullhorn, and set everything up. The first three days of the revival, there was a total of nine people who showed up. Of those nine people, none got saved. The man began to get a little worried that he may have misunderstood God. God said that he would save thousands! Where were they? So, day four came and two people showed up at the revival. Still, no one got saved. At this point, the man was upset and discouraged about the results of this "life changing" revival. Day five came and he told himself that he was going to complete what he thought God had told him to. He had already spent time and money to prepare for this revival for five days. That day during the revival, one man came. The only difference on this day was that this man did get saved. Praise God. One soul. The evangelist packed everything up and went home. Three years passed. One day the evangelist was sitting in his room watching television and flipping channels. He flipped to one particular channel and paused in disbelief. That very same man who came to his revival was on television saving thousands! Sometimes God can use strange methods that don't make sense to us to complete His purpose. This man is going to be rewarded for planting the seed and saving that one man which resulted in thousands being saved, which was God's harvest.

***Scripture point:** (Isaiah 55:8 NKJV) "For My thoughts are not your thoughts, nor are your ways My ways," says the Lord. "For as the heavens are higher than the earth, so are My ways higher than your ways, and My thoughts than your thoughts."*

Bulletin: Don't stop your work at every blessing thinking that one blessing is God's ultimate harvest.

DON'T QUIT!

11

Growing Pains of Potential

As you grow closer to achieving your full potential, you'll experience greater responsibility, greater challenges, but a greater reward. Remember how it felt when you went from kindergarten to grade school? In kindergarten, you had one teacher in one classroom and you had very little responsibility to make decisions for yourself. Your day was structured and dictated by your teacher, who determined what you did and when you did it. As you grew older and elevated to junior high and high school, you took on a greater level of responsibility for your actions and decisions. Now, you have multiple teachers in different classrooms and you have to be mature and responsible enough to move throughout your day with little oversight and direction. This is where your sense of accountability is tested. This is when you have the responsibility for making you own decisions, and dealing with the consequences of these decisions.

Just like it was in school, every level has a test to determine how much you've learned, and whether you're ready for the next grade. You're getting closer, and the tests are getting more difficult. Life, just like your school exams, gives you multiple choices, and if you're not careful and prayerful, you won't recognize the choice that was thrown in to trick you and to take you off course, especially when that choice looks as good as the others! Now I don't know about you, but when I took tests in school, the teacher didn't offer to help me take the test. She just prepared me for it. And that's how God works. Even through our trials and errors, He is building and preparing us for the test. But when it comes to making the right choices, we must take all that God has put in us and apply it to the test.

<u>Scripture point</u>: (Proverbs 3:5-6) Trust in the Lord with all your heart, and lean not on your own understanding; in all your ways acknowledge Him and He shall direct your paths.

If you go to God for help in all of your decisions, and allow the Holy Spirit to lead and guide you to the truth, you won't fall into the trap of the enemy and make the wrong choices. And despite the difficulty of the exam, you will pass the test. Just remember, if you never experience and overcome a negative situation, you won't gain the confidence for a positive one.

When you are confronted by the enemy and tempted to do something that goes against God's standards, what's in your heart will determine how you respond to the temptation. We can be easily persuaded to do wrong when what we believe is only in our minds. Our minds and our intellect were created to weigh and debate information. But, when it's planted in our hearts, nothing or no one can persuade or convince us to go against our conviction. That's why David says in ***Psalm 119:11***, "Your word I have hidden in my heart that I might not sin against You". You'll notice that David did not say that God's word was hidden in his mind, because he knew that his mind was not a secure enough place for such valuable information. But, once it was in his heart, he knew that it would guard and guide him to make the right choices.

You can always tell when someone has a conviction of the heart versus a conviction of the mind, because they are steadfast and immovable, and they can say no to themselves, and to others. There is a sector of the Jewish community who have such a heart conviction about the Sabbath, that no matter how logical or convenient it might be to go to the market, use their vehicles or use electricity, they cannot be convinced to do it because what they believe is firmly planted in their hearts.

Once it becomes a heart thing, it's not open for debate or compromise. And no one can convince you that what you know and believe isn't so. It's as simple as ketchup. Yes, ketchup! No matter how hard someone may try, there is no way for them to convince you that the red stuff in the bottle of concentrated tomatoes that you put on your hotdog is mustard. You know that it's ketchup. You've eaten it and you know what it tastes like. It's not just because what you know about ketchup is in your mind, but because the experience you've had with ketchup is in your heart and is no longer subject to debate. I know it sounds crazy, but that's how you have to be about God's word. You have to eat it so much that it becomes deeply rooted in your heart, and you can never be convinced that it's not true. And when it comes time to making a decision, you can't be bamboozled by cunning words and a convincing argument. You won't compromise.

DON'T QUIT!

12

They Can Only Get From You What They See

In building your potential, you must realize that some people won't see the growth of your potential. Some people won't want you to grow, and because of that, you can only become to them what they want you to be. In realizing this, your potential isn't built off of what other people believe, but what you believe in yourself.

Scripture point: ***(Matthew 13:53-58) Now it came to pass, when Jesus had finished these parables, that He departed from there. When He had come to His own country, He taught them in their synagogue, so that they were astonished and said, "Where did this Man get this wisdom and these mighty works? Is not this the carpenter's son? Is not His mother called Mary? And His brothers, James, Joses, Simon, and Judas? And His sisters, are they not all with us? Where then did this Man get all these things?" So they were offended at Him. But Jesus said to them, "A prophet is not without honor, except in his own country and in his own house."***

Jesus was such a great teacher, a great healer, a great visionary and more. However, the people from His old environment only acknowledged Him as Mary's son, the carpenter. They wanted to connect Him to where His brothers and sisters were then, locking Him into a community that wouldn't advance, and, were offended that He had advanced, but wouldn't accept it. Because of that, He couldn't do any good work. This didn't mean that He lacked the ability, but He wasn't afforded the opportunity to do these works. A similar example is growing up in a community and being around people that you have a love for, and they give you a nickname to stereotype where you are at that stage. But, as you begin to mature in your destiny, they continue to remind you of where you formerly were because of that one name, when life is filled with so many dimensions of who you are called to be.

***Scripture point:* (Mark 8:27-30) Now Jesus and His disciples went out to the towns of Caesarea Philippi; and on the road He asked His disciples, saying to them, "Who do men say that I am?" So they answered, "John the Baptist; but some say, Elijah; and others, one of the prophets." He said to them, "But who do you say that I am?" Peter answered and said unto Him, "You art the Christ." Then He strictly warned them that they should tell no one about Him.**

Sometimes in pushing toward your purpose, you will find people that will travel the distance with you but never see the change in you. They've already decided that you'll only have the ability to reach the potential that they saw in you when you started out with them. As Jesus began to ask the people who were with Him, "Who do *men* say that I am", they confirmed that men called Him John the Baptist or one of the prophets. But, when He asked them, "Who do ***you*** say that I am", all but one who traveled the distance and familiarized themselves with Jesus was unable to identify Him. The one exception was Peter, who identified Him as the Christ. That alone motivated Him to continue on. Sometimes you only need one. When your brothers and sisters may not see it, you just need one. You need that one old grandmother who knows the trouble you've been through to keep affirming what you're going to be. Sometimes, you need that one person that says, "I don't know what, where, when, why, or how but I see potential in you." That's the one that nobody listens or responds to because that one, that voice, that sound was designed to motivate your ears only. The majority is not always right. Strong movements were created and won by minorities. So, people will only receive from you what they see. Don't confirm yourself through every thing or person that is close to you. Sometimes you gain confirmation from the strangers in your life that stop by and pull ideas, joy, and peace out of you that your friends and family could never receive.

Some pastors base their level of success off of the size of their building and congregation. We should claim our success from fulfilling our purpose and design for what God has created us to be. No man's purpose is the same. God doesn't make carbon copies or duplicates. Don't get stuck looking at another man's work and reject your ultimate purpose.

So what if God didn't call you to be a bishop. So what if God didn't call you to be a doctor, lawyer, pastor, apostle or prophet. As long as He chose you to be. Many are called, but few are chosen ***(Matthew 20:16)***. The call does not confirm that you're going to be chosen. The call only means that you have the potential to be chosen. Most people respond to the call, but don't have patience to wait to be chosen. We have a lot of called bishops, doctors, pastors and lawyers, but, they have not been chosen. I'm not saying that you will not be chosen. I'm just saying that as Jesus was tempted in the wilderness, He was tempted by a premature manifestation of His purpose. Everything that satan offered Him was a part of His destiny, but it wasn't in God's perfect timing to accept it. Wait to be chosen. Don't move before your time. Your time will come.

DON'T QUIT!

13

Seven Keys To Effective Communication

In this chapter, I would like to give you seven powerful keys to effective communication. These keys are tools designed to strengthen and encourage positive communication that will lead you into a strong purpose.

***Scripture point*: (Proverbs 11:9) The hypocrite with his mouth destroys his neighbor, but through knowledge, the righteous will be delivered.**

One of the deficiencies people have in reaching their purpose is self expression. Positive communication can open many doors, while negative communication shuts doors that should be open. These seven keys will fortify your confidence in understanding that the things you feel, you can also express.

I must say this—If both parties utilize these seven keys in your personal relationship, your connection will develop and increase a great deal. However, if these keys are not being applied by both individuals, it will not produce *effective* communication. The ultimate goal is to work together to successfully communicate. Now let's begin.

***KEY 1*: KNOWING THE POWER OF WORDS**

Words can build you up, or words can tear you down. You must recognize and value the sensitivity and power of the words you relay to people. Positive words can encourage, push, and elevate a person, while, negative words will damage, discourage, and belittle a person. Learn to sow positive words into people, so that you can reap positive things. Always refrain from speaking negativity into the lives of others. What you speak to others can be very impacting. For example, there is a saying that has proven to be true: "Garbage in, garbage out." Don't sow negativity and expect a positive harvest.

Scripture points: ***(Proverbs 18:21) Death and life are in the power of the tongue, and those who love it will eat its fruit.***

(Proverbs 12:18) There is one who speaks like the piercings of a sword, but the tongue of the wise promotes health.

We as positive people must speak positive things, to encourage and push others to walk positively into their purpose. We must fulfill the will of God, and no longer damage and destroy people with our tongues because we don't understand or like who they are, or what they're doing. We must understand that God has created us to be the voice and the creation of His ultimate purpose. Any part of His purpose that our voice destroys through negative words will delay the plan, the vision, and the purpose of Almighty God in the earth. Say what Jesus said, do what Jesus did, and live how Jesus lived. He lived in love and died for love. Let's start talking in the language of God's love.

KEY 2: DISCERNING YOUR SOURCE

Before responding to any matters or concerns in your life, you must examine who or where the information comes from. In probing a person or addressing a matter, always consider every viewpoint and piece of information involved to determine where you stand. This will give you the confidence you need to be sure of your decisions.

Example: If you struggle with a heart condition, it would be wise to consult a heart surgeon regarding your options concerning medication or possible surgery. They will know the cause and effect of your condition, the pros and cons of surgery, and the side effects of any medications. Upon evaluation of your condition, they will be able to give you a factor of risk in whatever option you go with. But, if you seek counsel from a hairstylist, she can only give you the information of someone else's experience. She hears the information secondhand, but she's so passionate to influence you that the information is just as invaluable as that given by the heart surgeon. The first speaks from experience and the second speaks from hearsay.

Another common example of getting information from an unreliable source is, when you are lost and in need of directions to the closest highway that will lead you home, and you stop to ask a stranger to tell you the way. The stranger chooses to give you wrong directions without feeling guilty because they have already made up in their mind that they will never see you again. That source doesn't care because they feel that they will pay no price. People place their confidence in sources because of the convincing delivery of the information they're relaying without considering the consequences they will face in making bad decisions.

I found that most people would rather search for cheap information from someone that hasn't struggled, prepared, or endured an experience, rather than seek expensive counsel from someone who has paid the price to deposit information to push you into your purpose. Your source can make or break you. There is a difference between a landscaper and someone who just cuts grass. One cares for, treats, and maintains the lawn, while the other just cuts it to give the illusion of a job well done. Sometimes, the shortest route to a destination is not always the right route. Your source may give you a shortcut but mess your timing up. There is a thing that I have adopted in my church called dead truth. Learn your source. They may tell you the truth, but it's dead and buried. They may tell you information, but it's covered under the blood of Jesus. If you want a true source, make sure they have considered speaking to God before they speak to you. Discern your source!

KEY 3: LISTENING AND TAKING HEED

Through establishing communication, most people do not take heed. A lot of times during communication, a person will prepare their rebuttal before you finish your complete statement. Some people listen to the whole presentation of your opinion, and take one word and defend themselves off of ten percent of the entire information you have given them.

Example: There was a young lady, whose mother was telling her that she did not like the company she was with last night. She exposed all the things they did that night. She even told them that she saw them out. However, she made a mistake in the name of the street she said she saw them on. The daughter grabbed a hold of that one mistake and changed the whole argument from being about her lifestyle to defending herself and her whereabouts. Instead of admitting that she was wrong, she manipulated and altered the whole conversation so she wouldn't be put in a position of guilt. Most people don't mind admitting they're wrong as long as they can blame someone else and they don't stand alone when correction comes.

Scripture point: ***(James 1:19) So then, my beloved brethren, let every man be swift to hear, slow to speak, slow to wrath;***

When you admit you're wrong, you stop the judgment of the accuser against your purpose.

Scripture points: ***(Proverbs 10:19) In the multitude of words sin is not lacking, but he who restrains his lips is wise.***

(Proverbs 10:17) He who keeps instruction is in the way of life, but he who refuses correction goes astray.

(Proverbs 19:20) Listen to counsel and receive instruction, that you may be wise in your latter days.

A wise man will not protect his wrong, but admit it. Admitting that you're wrong will increase your knowledge. If you lie long enough, the liar will begin to believe his own lie. And that's the lie of a fool. Don't be anyone's fool!

KEY 4: REFRAIN FROM NAGGING

Scripture points: ***(Proverbs 21:19) Better to dwell in the wilderness, than with a contentious and angry woman.***

(Proverbs 26:21) As charcoal is to burning coals, and wood to fire, so is a contentious man to kindle strife.

Nagging is employed by the enemy to pull people out of their character. It is a force that can dominate people into a depressed state, where they are no longer strong-willed enough to stand on their own views. Nagging is a verbal form of abuse that eventually drives the other individual to lying. Nagging takes the other person out of their comfort zone, where they're no longer equal with the person doing the nagging. A person who nags is so determined to achieve their personal goal through nagging, that they don't consider who or what it will damage. It is better to allow a person to speak when they're ready, than to force them to speak under verbal imprisonment.

Example: Samson was nagged by Delilah so much that he lost his direction and purpose, his call and his sight. The first few incidents of Delilah nagging Samson lead him to lie because he was not in the position to share this information with Delilah. The last occurrence of her nagging him lead Samson to tell Delilah more information than she deserved to hear. He gave her information that blinded his whole purpose and destiny for his life ***(Judges 16:1-22)***. Here lies a man who has purpose in his belly, but no strength or fight to complete it, as the result of nagging. All because he had wrong conversation, wrong counsel, and was too quick to speak. If you're ever involved in a negative environment, just don't speak. Nagging is a vexing source of negative communication.

KEY 5: LYING BECAUSE OF FEAR

Restrain from lying at any cost. A major reason people are driven to lie is that they have fear of facing consequences that come with the truth. Normally, when someone lies out of fear, they never keep what is gained. It's best not to lie on applications, to salvage a relationship, to maintain an image, or, for any other reason. There shouldn't be one reason that justifies a lie. Not one. One thing about the truth is that it will free you ***(John 8:32)***. If I were to tell you I've never lied, that would be a lie. I will tell you that every lie accounted for required payment of an incredible price. A lie will cause you to lose something that you probably could have kept with your integrity. Lying discredits your integrity, therefore labeling you as untrustworthy.

Lying will break down and sometimes destroy positive communication. You can tell someone a lie, and because of the faith they have placed in your character, they will grasp and believe it. You lied to cover your fear, but the moment they find out you lied, that will make them second guess their ability to trust you in the future. As a result, the fear that you tried to cover has now become ten times stronger, and the person you lied to now has the authority to tell others that you are a liar. I'd rather be mocked for telling the truth, than to be mocked as a liar. Being free through the truth doesn't always feel good to your flesh, but it does feel good when people can stand on your character and integrity.

***Scripture points*: (Proverbs 12:22) Lying lips are an abomination to the Lord, but those who deal truthfully are His delight.**

(Psalm 34:13) Keep your tongue from evil, and your lips from speaking deceit.

(Proverbs 26:18-19) Like a madman who throws firebrands, arrows, and death, is the man who deceives his neighbor, and says, "I was only joking!"

Another person's destiny should be dealt with as delicately as you would have your destiny dealt with. Don't ever downplay the severity of a lie when dealing with a person's purpose. Remember to be careful of the words you speak to a person because it could blur a vision, or make them question God. The above scripture indicates that there are some people who lie, and then turn it around, as to say they were joking. If you lie to joke, joke to embarrass yourself instead of joking at the expense of someone else.

KEY 6: ADMITTING WHEN YOU'RE WRONG

Admitting when you're wrong is not a sickness, but an indication of maturity. It's a reminder that you're not always right. It destroys insecurity, it encourages others to admit when they're wrong, it shows that you have not taken a defensive position, and, you didn't come to battle, but reason. According to society, admitting that you're wrong is a sign of being a weak person. The good news is that God has a different outlook. When we admit that we're wrong, we humble ourselves in a position of lowliness, therefore allowing God to work with us.

Say this with me: "I was wrong, please forgive me." That didn't hurt did it?

Try this one: "You showed me the light of my dark view. I will no longer walk in ignorance. I accept my responsibility."

That wasn't bad was it?

Alright, let's try this one more time. Repeat after me: "How can I fix my wrong that I've done to you? I'm sorry."

Now right away, I've diffused the opposition by establishing that there is no room for battle. If the other party chooses to keep fighting, they must fight by themselves.

***Scripture point:** (Luke 15:11-20) Then He said: "A certain man had two sons. And the younger of them said to his father, 'Father, give me the portion of goods that falls to me.' So he divided to them his livelihood. And not many days after, the younger son gathered all together, journeyed to a far country, and there wasted his possessions with prodigal living. But when he had spent all, there arose a severe famine in that land, and he began to be in want. Then he went and joined himself to a citizen of that country, and he sent him into his fields to feed swine. And he would gladly have filled his stomach with the pods that the swine ate, and no one gave him anything. But when he came to himself, he said, 'How many of my father's hired servants have bread enough and to spare, and I perish with hunger! I will arise and go to my father, and will say to him, "Father, I have sinned against heaven and before you, and I am no longer worthy to be called your son. Make me like*

one of your hired servants.'" "And he arose and came to his father. But when he was still a great way off, his father saw him and had compassion, and ran and fell on his neck and kissed him."

(Matthew 5:25-26) Agree with your adversary quickly, while you are on the way with him, lest your adversary deliver you to the judge, the judge hand you over to the officer, and you be thrown into prison. Assuredly, I say to you, you will by no means get out of there till you have paid the last penny.

Admitting that you're wrong will raise Jesus up, but being prideful will allow satan the right to come in.

KEY 7: WALKING IN FORGIVENESS

This is the final key of effective communication. This is the hardest key, because in most situations, the person who has to walk in forgiveness is the person who has been wronged through negative communication. In this situation, you are right and according to man, you have every right to hold that person in imprisonment as a result of what they've said or done to you. However, being a Christian requires exceptions to the rules. In my ministry, there are several people that work as correctional officers. Every prison must have a guard to keep the prisoners locked up. When they go to work to guard the prisoners, they have to go through the same gates and bars that the prisoners go through. During their shift, they are enforcing the law by keeping the prisoners behind the bars. As long as they are confining the prisoners, they are in the same environment as them. When their shift is over and they are free to go, they are released from the gates and bars of the prison. Well, that same concept applies when you are dealing with someone who has wronged you. As long as you hold your offender in bondage for the wrong that they have done to you, every time you see or think about that person, you are losing your right to walk in joy, peace, contentment and freedom. In order to be free and clear with God, you have to apply the same ideas with the offender that God would with you. So, every time a person steps out to do something great and you remind them of the attack and damage they have done to you, you hold yourself and them in bondage.

BULLETIN: No one is perfect except God!

If God who is perfect can forgive us for how we have acted, neglected, treated and responded towards His own son Jesus Christ, then you can forgive someone else. The bible clearly makes an indisputable point by stating that if you hate your brother who you see everyday, than it would be impossible for you to love God who you don't see ***(1 John 4:20)***!

Walking in forgiveness is a practice, that must turn into a desire, that results in becoming a commandment. You must tell yourself, "I command myself to forgive them!" And why? Because of the scriptures below:

Scripture points: ***(Mark 11:25-26) "And whenever you stand in praying, if you have anything against anyone, forgive him, that your Father in heaven may also forgive you your trespasses. But if you do not forgive, neither will your Father in heaven forgive your trespasses."***

(Matthew 18:21-22) Then Peter came to Him saying, "Lord, how often shall my brother sin against me, and I forgive him? Up to seven times?" Jesus said to him, "I do not say to you, up to seven times, but up to seventy times seven."

These two scriptures speak for themselves. Walking in forgiveness will give you the right to move into another position. Forgiveness does not mean that I give you the right to do it again, or the right to be tested in the same area again, but it means that I no longer judge you for what you've done to me. It also gives me the right to change my position in peace, not anger, so you won't do it again.

Scripture point: ***(Romans 12:17-19) Repay no one evil for evil. Have regard for good things in the sight of all men. If it is possible, as much as depends on you, live peaceably with all***

men. Beloved, do not avenge yourselves, but rather give place to wrath; for it is written, "Vengeance is Mine, I will repay," says the Lord.

Isn't it good to know that every time you walk in forgiveness, God will repay *you* for what your enemy has done to you?

I've given you seven keys to apply:

1. Knowing the power of words
2. Discerning your source
3. Listening and taking heed
4. Refrain from nagging
5. Lying because of fear
6. Admitting when you're wrong
7. Walking in forgiveness

I stated earlier that if the two parties don't agree to do these things together, then they won't be effective. Now, I am going to give you a way to master all seven keys by making one of these keys your focal point. Are you ready? Ok, make a note of this:

The key to master in order to allow the other keys to fall in line is ***walking in forgiveness***. If you master the key to walking in forgiveness, you can master all of the other keys. This is all a part of you possessing your purpose. Avoiding this chapter may lead to many downfalls.

DON'T QUIT!

14

The Process of Your Purpose

PART 1 - FIND GOD IN IT

Every purpose must come with a process. If you accept your purpose, you cannot reject your process. Before becoming a pastor, and as a pastor, I have found that there are very few people that won't accept their purpose, but most people will reject their process.

Scripture point: ***(Matthew 20:16) "So the last will be first, and the first last. For many are called, but few chosen."***

You were only chosen after the process. During a pregnant woman's final hour in labor, she prepares to push out a destiny. As the contractions increase, so does the pain. When the pain reaches a level that she feels she is unequipped to handle, she requests a pain reliever, or an epidural. The doctor will agree to give the mother some relief, so he prepares to place a needle in the mother's lower back. Before administering the shot, he cautions her that this procedure requires her full cooperation in sitting still because with the slightest wrong movement, it may result in paralysis. The doctor now has the ability to alleviate the pain, but damage a future. He carefully slides the needle precisely in her back. As the mother is sitting and waiting, she begins to feel partly relieved from the excruciating pain of the contractions. After the contraction passes, she looks at the doctor requesting more medication. The doctor responds by telling her that he can't give her any more relief, because if he does, when it is time to push, she won't be able to and won't have the desire to.

The process brings pain to deliver your purpose. In your process, you may get a little relief, but you will always end up with some pain. In this chapter, I will give you scriptures to distinguish different types of processes to lead into purpose. Nobody has the same process. There are pastors, prophets, ministers, elders, evangelists and so forth that may have the same title, but different processes. Now let's begin.

***Scripture point*: (Proverbs 3:5-6) Trust in the Lord with all your heart, and lean not on your own understanding; In all your ways acknowledge Him, and He shall direct your paths.**

It doesn't matter how hard the process is. God has planned to mold you into something great. Remember Job? One day, satan decided that he wanted to go and visit God. God asks satan where he was coming from. Satan answered God and told Him, oh I was just walking around (really meaning he wanted to find somebody to mess with). So, God asked satan if he considered going to Job. Now, that may sound a little strange, right? Well, God always has a plan behind everything He says and does. God used satan to attack Job, so that He could mold Job into the man of great faith that he is today. Sometimes to establish your character, you need to find God in your disaster and in your tears. ***Philippians 13:3-15*** says only mature people will seek God instead of complaining. If you ask God to be a healer, He may allow you to get sick. If you ask God for wealth, He may allow you to file for bankruptcy. If you ask God to be a mother, He may put you in a position to baby-sit unruly children for the weekend. Your flesh is designed to accept your purpose, but alter your process. So friend, press on by finding God in everything you do.

***Scripture point*: (Psalm 37:23-31) The steps of a good man are ordered by the Lord, and He delights in his way. Though he fall, he shall not be utterly cast down; For the Lord upholds him with His hand. I have been young, and now am old; yet I have not seen the righteous forsaken, nor His descendants begging bread. He is ever merciful, and lends; and His**

descendants are blessed. Depart from evil, and do good; and dwell forevermore. For the Lord loves justice, and does not forsake His saints; they are preserved forever. But the descendants of the wicked shall be cut off. The righteous shall inherit the land, and dwell in it forever. The mouth of the righteous speaks wisdom. And his tongue talks of justice. The law of his God is in his heart; none of his steps shall slide.

If God ordained it, don't reject it, just receive all of it.

<u>Let's study the process of Jesus:</u>

During Jesus' process, He was ready to fulfill His purpose, but the process was not complete.

(Luke 2:41-49) His parents went to Jerusalem every year at the feast of the Passover. And when He was twelve years old, they went up to Jerusalem according to the custom of the feast. When they had finished the days, as they returned, the boy Jesus lingered behind in Jerusalem. And Joseph and His mother did not know it: but supposing Him to have been in the company, they went a day's journey, and sought Him among their relatives and acquaintances. So when they did not find Him, they returned to Jerusalem, seeking Him. Now so it was that after three days they found Him in the temple, sitting in the midst of the teachers, both listening to them and asking them questions. And all who heard Him were astonished at His understanding and answers. So when they saw Him, they were amazed; and His mother said to him, "Son, why have You done this to us? Look, Your father and I have sought You anxiously." And He said to them, "Why did you seek Me? Did you not know that I must be about My Father's business?"

Jesus builds the confidence of the people to fulfill His process.

(John 11:41-42) Then they took away the stone from the place where the dead man was lying. And Jesus lifted up His eyes and said, "Father, I thank You that You have heard Me. And I

know that You always hear Me, but because of the people who are standing by I said this, that they may believe that You sent Me."

Jesus won't let anyone alter His process.

(Luke 22:49-53) When those around Him saw what was going to happen, they said to Him, "Lord, shall we strike with the sword?" And one of them struck the servant of the high priest and cut off his right ear. But Jesus answered and said, "Permit even this." And He touched his ear and healed him. Then Jesus said to the chief priests, captains of the temple, and the elders who had come to Him, "Have you come out, as against a robber, with swords and clubs? When I was with you daily in the temple you did not try to seize Me. But this is your hour, and the power of darkness."

This declares that every process comes with pain.

(Mark 14:34-36) Then He said to them, "My soul is exceedingly sorrowful, even to death. Stay here and watch." He went a little farther, and fell on the ground, and prayed that if it were possible, the hour might pass from Him. And He said "Abba, Father, all things are possible for You. Take this cup away from Me; nevertheless, not what I will, but what You will."

Jesus couldn't be forced into His process, but He had to surrender to it.

(John 10:17-18) "Therefore My Father loves Me, because I lay down My life that I may take it again. No one takes it from Me, but I lay it down of myself. I have power to lay it down, and I have power to take it again. This command I have received from My Father."

In every process, there is a time of forgiveness.

(Luke 23:34) Then Jesus said, "Father, forgive them, for they do not know what they do." And they divided His garments and cast lots.

This process is transitioning Jesus to walk in His purpose.

(Luke 23:46) And when Jesus had cried out with a loud voice, He said, "Father, 'into Your hands I commit My spirit.'" Having said this, He breathed His last.

As Jesus walked in His purpose, His purpose allowed Him to strengthen the weaker brethren.

(John 20:25-29) The other disciples therefore said to him, "We have seen the Lord." So he said to them, "Unless I see in His hands the print of the nails, and put my finger into the print of the nails, and put my hand into His side, I will not believe." And after eight days His disciples were again inside, and Thomas with them. Jesus came, the doors being shut, and stood in the midst, and said, "Peace to you!" Then He said to Thomas, "Reach your finger here, and look at My hands; and reach your hand here, and put it into My side. Do not be unbelieving, but believing." And Thomas answered and said to Him, "My Lord and my God!" Jesus said to him, "Thomas, because you have seen Me, you have believed. Blessed are those who have not seen and yet have believed."

This is just a portion of Jesus' process to win a people back to God.

PART 2 - THE FRUSTRATION OF YOUR PURPOSE

It would be nice to tell you that when God gives you a purpose, angels begin to sing, trumpets begin to sound, and the earth begins to open up to sing praises for you accepting your purpose. Unfortunately, it doesn't quite work out like that. When you accept your purpose, God assigns intercessors to pray on your behalf, because there is definitely going to be some frustration in your purpose. Keep in mind that every man's purpose is not the same. Your frustration may be timing, while someone else's frustration can be the feeling of void and loneliness.

<u>Scripture point</u>: (Ezra 4:1-5) Now when the adversaries of Judah and Benjamin heard that the descendants of the captivity were building the temple of the Lord God of Israel, they came to Zerubbabel and the heads of the fathers' housed, and said to them, "Let us build with you, for we seek your God as you do; and we have sacrificed to Him since the days of Esarhaddon king of Assyria, who brought us here." But Zerubabbel and Jeshua and the rest of the heads of the fathers' houses of Israel said to them, "You may do nothing with us to build a house for our God; but we alone will build to the Lord God of Israel, as King Cyrus the king of Persia has commanded us." Then the people of the land tried to discourage the people of Judah. They troubled them in building, and hired counselors against them to frustrate their purpose all the days of Cyrus king of Persia, even until the reign of Darius king of Persia.

When you are in line to do the will of God, there are people, spirits, and environments to frustrate your purpose. That frustration will determine how entangled and in love you are with your purpose. If you're not in love with it, you won't keep it. When you find your purpose, eventually you will also find people who are in your present, but are not assigned to be a part of your future. The purpose of your frustration is to train you in patience and trust the God inside of you. Frustration is also intended to kill the old man in you in order to birth the man that God has shaped within you. All frustration is not provoked by the devil. There is some frustration that no one but you had anything to do with. Some people have said, "I'm going to do your will God, but I'm not going to like it." In frustration, patience is the remedy. There's a saying, "If you're going to pray, don't worry and if you're going to worry, don't pray." I'd rather pray, than worry. I'd like to show you an example of someone getting frustrated in their purpose.

<u>***The frustration during Jonah's process***</u>

Jonah denied his process.

(Jonah 1:1-3) Now the word of the Lord came to Jonah the son of Amittai, saying, "Arise, go to Nineveh, that great city, and cry out against it; for their wickedness has come up before Me." But Jonah arose to flee to Tarshish from the presence of the Lord. He went down to Joppa, and found a ship going to Tarshish; so he paid the fare, and went down into it, to go with them to Tarshish from the presence of the Lord.

By denying his process, Jonah affects everyone's purpose.

(Jonah 1:4-16) But the Lord sent out a great wind on the sea, and there was a mighty tempest on the sea, so that the ship was about to be broken up. Then the mariners were afraid; and every man cried out to his god, and threw the cargo that was in the ship into the sea, to lighten the load. But Jonah had gone down, and was fast asleep. So the captain came to him, and said to him, "What do you mean, sleeper? Arise, call on your God; perhaps your God will consider us, so that we many not perish" And they said to one another, "Come, let us cast lots, that we may know for whose cause this trouble has come upon us." So they cast lots, and the lot fell on Jonah. Then they said to him, "Please tell us! For whose cause is this trouble upon us? What is your occupation? And where do you come from? What is your country? And of what people are you?" So he said to them, "I am a Hebrew; and I fear the Lord, the God of heaven, who made the sea and the dry land." Then the men were exceedingly afraid, and said to him, "Why have you done this?" For the men knew that he fled from the presence of the Lord, because he had told them. Then they said to him, "What shall we do to you that the sea may be calm for us?" For the sea was growing more tempestuous. And he said to them, "Pick me up and throw me into the sea; then the sea will become calm for you. For I know that this great tempest is because of

me." Nevertheless the men rowed hard to return to land, but they could not, for the sea continued to grow more tempestuous against them. Therefore they cried out to the Lord and said, "We pray, O Lord, please do not let us perish for this man's life, and do not charge us with innocent blood; for you, O Lord, have done as it pleased You." So they picked up Jonah and threw him into the sea, and the sea ceased from its raging. Then the men feared the Lord exceedingly, and offered a sacrifice to the Lord and took vows.

As long as Jonah denied his process, he stayed stuck.

(Jonah 1:17) Now the Lord had prepared a great fish to swallow Jonah. And Jonah was in the belly of the fish three days and three nights.

(Jonah 2:1-10)Then Jonah prayed to the Lord his God from the fish's belly. And he said: "I cried out to the Lord because of my affliction, And He answered me. Out of the belly of Sheol I cried, And You heard my voice. For You cast me into the deep, Into the heart of the seas, And the floods surrounded me; All Your billows and Your waves passed over me. Then I said, 'I have been cast out of Your sight; Yet I will look again toward Your holy temple.' The waters surrounded me, even to my soul; The deep closed around me; Weeds were wrapped around my head. I went down to the moorings of the mountains; The earth with its bars closed behind me forever; Yet you have brought up my life from the pit, O Lord , my God. When my soul fainted within me, I remembered the Lord; And my prayer went up to You, into Your holy temple. Those who regard worthless idols forsake their own mercy. But I will sacrifice to You with the voice of thanksgiving; I will pay what I have vowed. Salvation is of the Lord." So the Lord spoke to the fish, and it vomited Jonah onto dry land.

Even though Jonah didn't like it, as a part of his process, he still had to follow through with his assignment.

(Jonah 3:1-4) Now the word of the Lord came to Jonah the second time, saying, "Arise, go to Nineveh, that great city, and preach to it the message that I tell you." So Jonah arose and went to Nineveh, according to the word of the Lord. Now Nineveh was an exceedingly great city, a three-day journey in extent. And Jonah began to enter the city on the first day's walk. Then he cried out and said, "Yet forty days, and Nineveh shall be overthrown!"

Jonah fulfills his process leading to his purpose.

(Jonah 3:5-10) So the people of Nineveh believed God, proclaimed a fast, and put on sackcloth, from the greatest to the least of them. Then word came to the king of Nineveh; and he arose from his throne and laid aside his robe, covered himself with sackcloth and sat in ashes. And he caused it to be proclaimed and published throughout Nineveh by the decree of the king and his nobles, saying, "Let neither man nor beast, herd nor flock, taste anything; do not let them eat, or drink water. But let man and beast be covered with sackcloth, and cry mightily to God; yes, from the violence that is in his hands. Who can tell if God will turn and relent, and turn away from His fierce anger, so that we may not perish?" Then God saw their works, that they turned from their evil way; and God relented from the disaster that He had said He would bring upon them, and He did not do it.

Jonah fulfills his process, but mentally refuses to leave the belly of the whale.

(Jonah 4:1-11) But it displeased Jonah exceedingly, and he became angry. So he prayed to the Lord, and said, "Ah, Lord, was not this what I said when I was still in my country? Therefore I fled previously to Tarshish; for I know that You are a gracious and merciful God, slow to anger and abundant in lovingkindness, One who relents from doing harm. "Therefore now, O Lord, please take my life from me, for it is better for me

to die than to live!" Then the Lord said, "Is it right for you be angry?" So Jonah went out of the city and sat on the east side of the city. There he made himself shelter and sat under it in the shade, till he might see what would become of the city. So Jonah was very grateful for the plant. But as morning dawned the next day God prepared a worm, and it so damaged the plant that it withered. And it happened, when the sun arose, that God prepared a vehement east wind; and the sun beat on Jonah's head, so that he grew faint. Then he wished death for himself, and said, "It is better for me to die than to live." Then God said to Jonah, "Is it right for you to be angry about the plant?" "And he said, "It is right for me to be angry, even to death!" But the Lord said, "You have had pity on the plant for which you have not labored, nor made it grow, which came up in a night and perished in a night. "And should I not pity Nineveh, that great city, in which are more than one hundred and twenty thousand persons who cannot discern between their right hand and their left--and much livestock?"

***Scripture point*: (James 1:2-4) My brethren, count it all joy when you fall into various trials, knowing that the testing of your faith produces patience. But let patience have its perfect work, that you may be perfect and complete, lacking nothing.**

PART 3 - IT'S NOT REJECTION BUT DIRECTION

In most cases, people feel that any type of rebuke or chastening is a sign of rejection. They pray and pray and pray, and when God doesn't respond fast enough for them, they think that He is rejecting them. Sometimes silence is a way to direct you, not reject you. In ***Hebrews 12:5-6***, the writer personally says God chastens and chastises those He loves.

When I was a child, maybe between the ages of 2-3, while curiously finding my way through the room, I would reach for the electrical outlet to pull any plugs out. My mother would reach for me and move me away from the outlet, and explain to me why I shouldn't do that.

Her reasoning was because it would harm me. But when I got older between the ages of 4-5, I would do the same thing, but this time the process of correction was different because more was expected of me. My mom would still reach for me and move me away from the outlet, but now instead of explaining why I shouldn't do it, she would chastise me. As you age, you should be declaring maturity. Now, being a grown man, if I reach for the outlet, my mother would not do or say anything because she knows now that if I knowingly decide to do something that will require me to pay the price, then I am grown enough to handle the penalty that comes with it.

At some ages, God says, don't do that. Then, He begins to put more pressure on you. If you keep doing the same thing, God gets silent, and it feels as though you are neglected because He didn't stop you before your pain. Sometimes, the only way that people in the body of Christ will learn is through experience, not revelation.

In ***Mark 9:17-29***, the man brings his son to the disciples. These are the same disciples that saw miraculous works through Jesus' hands. The disciples referred to Jesus as "Rabbi" (teacher). That declares that Jesus was teaching the disciples every function of His ministry. It also indicates that Jesus created a line of protocol to get this man's son healed. But, those who were in position were not in order. As a result of them being out of order, the man went to Jesus and said I went through protocol, but Your disciples could not do what You taught them, so Jesus had to heal the man's son. After this was over, the disciples came to Him privately and asked Him why they couldn't heal the boy. Jesus responded by telling them that they chose to be like Him, but they refused to go through the process to be like Him. This is not rejection, but Jesus had to show the disciples that you must be pushed into the call, because if you don't fulfill the process, the purpose won't work.

Sometimes in fulfilling our purpose, when we can't identify direction, we automatically assume rejection has set in. God allowed Elisha to go through a process that may have seemed like rejection, but it was only for his direction.

<u>Let's look at Elisha's process for the direction of his purpose.</u>

Elijah tells Elisha that he has to depart

(2 Kings 2:1-2) And it came to pass, when the Lord was about to take up Elijah into heaven by a whirlwind, that Elijah went with Elisha from Gilgal. Then Elijah said to Elisha, "Stay here, please, for the Lord has sent me on to Bethel." But Elisha said, "As the Lord lives, and as your soul lives, I will not leave you!" So they went down to Bethel.

Elisha rebukes the prophets in order to accept his process

(2 Kings 2:5) Now the sons of the prophets who were at Jericho came to Elisha and said to him, "Do you know that the Lord will take away your master from over you today?" So he answered, "Yes, I know; keep silent!"

Elijah instructs Elisha to go back, but Elisha chooses to complete the process to receive his purpose

(2 Kings 2:6) Then Elijah said to him, "Stay here, please, for the Lord has sent me on to the Jordan." But he said, "As the Lord lives, and as your soul lives, I will not leave you!" So the two of them went on.

Elisha requests a double portion of the anointing

(2 Kings 2:9) And so it was, when they had crossed over, that Elijah said to Elisha, "Ask! What may I do for you, before I am taken away from you?" Elisha said, "Please let a double portion of your spirit be upon me."

Elisha accepts the separation from his master

(2 Kings 2:12) And Elisha saw it, and he cried out, "My father, my father, the chariot of Israel and its horsemen!" So he saw

him no more. And he took hold of his own clothes and tore them into two pieces.

Elisha receives the mantle to fulfill direction

(2 Kings 2:13-14) He also took up the mantle of Elijah that had fallen from him, and went back and stood by the bank of the Jordan. Then he took the mantle of Elijah that had fallen from him, and struck the water, and said, "Where is the Lord God of Elijah?" And when he also had struck the water, it was divided this way and that; and Elisha crossed over.

Elisha fulfills his process to obtain a double portion of the anointing

(2 Kings 2:15) Now when the sons of the prophets who were from Jericho saw him, they said, "The spirit of Elijah rests on Elisha." And they came to meet him, and bowed to the ground before him.

PART 4 - "DON'T TOUCH ME"

One of the things that I've discovered in going through the process of my purpose is that, you go through a season in which you can't be touched. It feels like you can't be reached, helped, or supported. That brings me to ***John 20:15-17***, when Mary comes to seek Jesus' body. There's a time in your life when people come and seek you. As they are seeking you, they are looking for the same, familiar person that you used to be, not knowing that now you are walking in a different place, being a different person, with a different attitude, and a different response. They don't recognize you in the spirit, just as Mary didn't recognize Jesus, and called Him a gardener. Your language, desire, and focus will be elevated to a greater level, with a greater call, and a greater direction and purpose. In that time of your life, you cannot be touched. Just as Mary reached out for Jesus, He responded in verse 17 telling her not to touch Him, because He had not yet ascended to His Father. You need to understand that people cannot touch you in certain areas and seasons of your life.

People have the ability to pull you back into a grave (dead) situation. That is the period in your life where you feel you've received great illumination of where God is taking you and where you are going, but no one can see or receive you. As a pastor, this reminds me of the times God has told me to do crazy, unorthodox, and peculiar things. I would go to my leadership and begin to tell them the vision and plan of the realm the church is moving to, and by the expressions on their faces and the comments made, they questioned the timing and reason. That clearly told me where I was in my purpose then. I could not allow people to touch me, and I was standing by myself. I couldn't be afraid of their faces. Not just the face of rejection, but sometimes the face of fear. You have to be like Jesus and tell the disciples to meet you in the upper room. In my case, I tell my leadership to prepare the people to receive me, because when I come back from prayer, fasting, and seeking the Lord, I can't allow you to touch the vision and alter it while you run with it. The phrase, "Don't touch me" doesn't make me superior, it just means that I haven't finished going through the process of metamorphosis. This way I can be confident in my faith that if God said it, that settles it!

<u>Scripture point</u>: (1 Chronicles 16:21-22 NKJV) He permitted no man to do them wrong; yes, He rebuked kings for their sakes, saying, "Do not touch My anointed ones, and do My prophets no harm."

I'd like to caution you to be very careful of who and what you touch in dealing with protocol during the journey of walking in your process to fulfill your purpose. When a man or woman has a call of God on their life, and God allows them to have a title of authority in His office, they become property of God. They should surrender their life, mind, and soul to God. We, as the body, can't be like the world. We must learn not to touch God's anointed. We need to be careful to keep our mouths and actions off of God's anointed. It doesn't matter if we feel that they are totally out of order. They're not our property, but God's property, and God will deal with them the way He sees fit. God will deal with you if you take His job dealing with them. The bible says,

"Touch not My anointed ones and do My prophet no harm." My mind goes back to the bible and how David struggled with Saul. Saul chose to attack David because Saul fell into flesh. David had all power to humiliate Saul, to expose Saul, and to kill Saul, but David chose not to touch him because he was the property of God. It is wise to let a parent punish their child, but foolish for an outsider to touch what he never created. When the outsider touches the child, he not only has war with the child, but also with the daddy. My suggestion is, if you find or see any of God's property out of line or misusing their authority, don't create a committee to express or destroy what is wrong in your eyes, but take him to his Father, because his Father can do more than you ever could. His Father holds his birthright.

Scripture points*:** ***(Psalm 105:14-15 NKJV) He permitted no one to do them wrong; yes, He rebuked kings for their sakes, saying, "Do not touch My anointed ones, and do My prophets no harm."

(2 Samuel 6:5-7 NKJV) Then David and all the house of Israel played music before the Lord on all kinds of instruments of fir wood, on harps, on stringed instruments, on tambourines, on sistrums, and on cymbals. And when they came to Nachon's threshing floor, Uzzah put out his hand to the ark of God and took hold of it, for the oxen stumbled. Then the anger of the Lord was aroused against Uzzah, and God struck him there for his error; and he died there by the ark of God.

This scripture begins to show Uzzah, (which means strength), taking his strength and touching God's anointed to support it. As the oxen stumbled with the ark, Uzzah reaches out his hand to touch the ark, and God's whole plan was to help hold the ark up in a stumbling situation. Keep in mind, that in dealing with God's anointed, whatever process God takes the anointed through, we can't touch it. Even though Uzzah took his strength to hold it up, God killed him because He controlled the ark and the oxen. What we call a stumble was God's plan.

Before starting my ministry, I governed hundreds of people in another ministry. When I started my ministry, I had sixteen people. There were many days I looked for help from pastors and friends I was well acquainted with, prior to becoming a pastor. I searched and searched, but I couldn't find strength. Forty five days later, sixteen members dwindled down to eight people, who assembled in a building large enough to hold a capacity of five hundred. I had no idea that this was God's plan, that the oxen would stumble to get me to the destination where I am today, with several properties, a large ministerial staff, and a host of members. During the process, I couldn't understand why no one wanted to touch me. I didn't know that every stumble I made was God's will, and He didn't allow the people that I thought could help me not to reach out and touch me at all. That's why I can say glory be to God for everything that I have accomplished up to this day. It doesn't mean that you won't get people to touch you. Your path may be different. My path was written just for *me* and your path will be written just for *you*!

DON'T QUIT!

15

It May Be Formed, But It Won't Win

Like it or not, there are things you have to go through to become who you are before the glory of God can be revealed in you. I know that sounds unpleasant, and may even cause you to fear, but just remember that God said He would always be with you—even when you're going through.

Scripture point: ***(Psalm 23:4 NKJV) Yea, though I walk through the valley of the shadow of death, I will fear no evil; for You are with me.***

On your way to realizing your potential, weapons will rise against you. Those weapons may include painful words, distressing circumstances, and perhaps even challenges in your

health or finances. The one thing that you must remember when the enemy rises against you in any area of your life, is that the weapon may be formed—but it won't win. Yes, that's right. There will be weapons and there will be attacks, but they won't win!

Scripture point: ***(Isaiah 54:17 NKJV) No weapon formed against you shall prosper, and every tongue which rises against you in judgment You shall condemn.***

In other words, when you are purpose-driven, weapons will be formed, but they can't take you out. Notice that the scripture doesn't say that weapons won't exist. Sometimes, the weapon comes in the form of the aging process of our physical bodies to cause us to slow down or even stop. This weapon gives the illusion of an inability to reach our full potential, but when we realize that God still has purpose for us, we will not let any weapon, not even our physical bodies stop us from fulfilling it. Weapons are formed to teach and remind us that we shouldn't hit the "pause" button when something comes up against us. We shouldn't put our potential on hold because of one bad relationship or some other misfortune.

> ***BULLETIN:*** Don't let one emotion direct or affect a lifetime of purpose. Don't be like Samson and let your emotions blind you to the point that it affects your purpose. Shake it off!

Have you ever gone through something that initially looked impossible, but later you realized that it wasn't as bad as you thought? That's because we fail to realize that the measure of greatness within us far outweighs, and, has the power to conquer any situation we may be faced with. Don't ever let a temporary situation affect a permanent decision. Don't let fear get in the way of your faith. Remember, God is with you.

***Scripture point:* (1 John 4:4 NKJV) You are of God, little children and have overcome them, because He who is in you is greater than he who is in the world.**

You see, it's the enemy's plan to use his weapon to take you off course and to destroy your destiny and purpose. But you must remember, your steps are ordered by God—a*ll of them!*

***Scripture point:* (Hebrews 13:5 NKJV) ...For He Himself has said, "I will never leave you nor forsake you".**

Even though you may not "feel" His presence, your faith should remind you that He is there. When you're going through an attack, God will test you to see if you'll make the right decisions, or if you will revert back to your old ways. Will you continue to pray, call on God, and give Him praise? Or, will you use *your* tongue as a weapon for complaining and whining? Your mind is the ultimate battleground for any warfare, particularly one that uses words as weapons. But remember, you can choose whether or not to let the words hurt you. Just make up in your mind that no weapon formed against you shall prosper, and every tongue that rises against you God will condemn.

BULLETIN: Don't make your season of pity a career. It's alright to go through it, but don't make it your life.

For example, maybe you went through a painful situation five years ago, when someone you loved betrayed you, hurt you, or perhaps cheated on you! I know it hurt, and you had every right to go through a season of disappointment and tears. However, if you are still talking about that person or situation, and having frequent "pity parties" about it, you've gotten stuck. You've made a career out of feeling sorry for yourself, and you will drag those people around you into your pity party. Believe me, the whining and "oh me" syndrome gets boring to the listener, especially when there's nothing they can do to help you. If God ordained you to go through this, no one can get you out of, except God.

The scripture ***Isaiah 54:17*** also talks about the tongues that will rise against you that God will condemn. Several of our attacks come from the words that are spoken against us, and often from people who don't know your purpose or potential. But woe unto them, for God said that He would condemn *every* tongue that says you won't make it, and every person that will try to stop you from reaching your potential. So, if God said that He would take care of it, why are you dealing with it? Why are you seeking revenge and condemnation for those who are speaking against you?

Scripture points:* *(Ephesians 6:12 NKJV) For we do not wrestle against flesh and blood, but against principalities, against powers, against the rulers of the darkness of this age, against spiritual hosts of wickedness in the heavenly places.

(Romans 12:19 NKJV) Beloved, do not avenge yourselves, but rather give place to wrath; for it is written, "Vengeance is Mine, I will repay," says the Lord.

God will repay you for enduring the attack in His name. Just remember, it's not your battle. Don't look at the person or people who are attacking you, but look at the spirit of the weapon. When it's all said and done, those same tongues will have to recognize the God in you, and give Him praise for you. You can't waste your time or your energy worrying about talkers. You'll never catch up with all of them. Rather than trying to chase the talkers down and prove to them that they're wrong, use that time to develop your praise and communion with God. It seems like only in times of tragedy and disaster do we develop a more mature praise and prayer life. I call it the "intensive care prayer." That's when we feel so overwhelmed by the weapon that we can't physically praise God or pray, and all we can do is call on the Holy Spirit to speak for us.

***Scripture point:* (Romans 8:26 NKJV) Likewise the Spirit also helps in our weaknesses. For we do not know what we should pray for as we ought, but the Spirit Himself makes intercession for us with groanings which cannot be uttered.**

Thank God for the Holy Spirit! Only He can bring us the peace and relief when the issues come against us. When we're going through the battle, no man, woman, money, or material possession can bring you relief. Only God can. I recently had the opportunity to hear the testimony of a Muslim brother who was shot and nearly killed. He said that the teachings of Islam made him feel like a man, but when tragedy struck, it wasn't manhood that he was concerned about. He knew that he needed something more, he needed life. He didn't call on Muhammad, but he said, "I called on the God of my mother, Jesus Christ!" What he realized was, there is only one true and living God, and only He can stop the weapon from destroying you.

***Scripture point:* (Psalm 124:1 NKJV) If it had not been for the Lord who was on our side….**

Selah. Think about it.

What would have happened, or where would you be if it had not been for the Lord saving you, rescuing you, delivering you? If the Lord had not been on your side when your mother and father forsook you, or when you hung around the wrong crowd, where would you be today?

The only reason you made it through storms is because God was with you every step of the way. Everyday God allowed a small portion of light to radiate in the dark situations of your life.

***Scripture point:** (Psalm 27:10 NKJV) When my father and my mother forsake me, then the Lord will take care of me.*

Perhaps your testimony is of another nature. Maybe it was a financial hardship, the loss of a loved one through death or divorce, or perhaps it was unforeseen danger caused by someone you called best friend. Whatever the battle was, just take a moment to reflect—if it had not been for the Lord who was on my side! That ought to send you into a praise because although the weapon was formed, it didn't prosper. It didn't destroy you. Now, the people who judged you when they saw the weapon must judge you from your victory. You are more than a conqueror.

> ***BULLETIN:*** Victory doesn't come from what we go through but from the position we're going in.

God has a plan for everything that comes in our life—even the weapons.

When people attack you with their tongues it's either out of jealousy or because they were given false information and believed it. That's why you have to see the spirit of the weapon and not the person using the weapon. You must understand the principle of "cause and effect", so that you don't fight against the person, but against the spirit.

***Scripture point:** (2 Corinthians 10:4 NKJV) For the weapons of our warfare are not carnal but mighty in God for pulling down strongholds.*

Wow! That is powerful. What God is saying, is that, while the enemy may have a weapon to attack us, the weapons we have are more powerful and effective because they come directly from God. The enemy's devices don't stand a chance against the almighty God. So, why are we worried, stressed out and defeated? If the weapon won't win, then why are we losing? I'll tell you why—it's because we become our own weapon, our own enemy. God gets us out, but we keep going back in. If we're going to call on God for help, we must trust Him and follow His commands.

When I was a child, a pot of boiling water fell all over me and I suffered third degree burns as a result of this. The burns had damaged much of my face and my chest. The doctor said that they would have to remove skin from other parts of my body to do what is known as a skin graft. My body temperature was so high, that I can remember seeing steam rising from my chest. After hearing from the doctors about this surgery I'd need, and that I would have permanent scarring and other physical problems, my mother broke down and cried. But, if it had not been for the Lord on my side! The Lord sent one of His messengers, in the person of Mother Peterson, to my hospital room, and she declared to the doctors, my mother, and me, that not a piece of my skin would be removed, and that God Himself would heal and restore my body back to perfect health. She knew even before I did that I had a destiny and a call of God on my life, and that no weapon was going to destroy me. Now, many years later, there's no physical evidence of this tragic accident. No scarring. No related health problems. No fears. All because the Lord was on my side. Remember, He already knows what you're going through before you even go through it. Your victory plan is already written. Now it's up to you to stick to the script, even when you don't understand.

What do I mean by "the script" you may ask? The script is the preordained plan that God designed for the body of Christ to follow. The script is the written footsteps of your process. The script reflects God's principles and His order, respecting protocol and those who He has placed in authority over you. It is critical that you stay in your role, and not judge or attack the other "characters" in the script that God ordained to pressure and push you into your purpose. This is where we usually mess up because we don't like to be pushed and we don't like to submit to authority. So, we'll walk away from the script, leave the church, our jobs, our relationships, our responsibilities, or whatever place that is designed to push us, because we have no tolerance for persecution. We ought to be like David was when he was being persecuted by Saul. Saul sought to kill David, but instead of retaliating and attacking Saul, David realized that Saul was a part of God's order that would lead him to his purpose. That's the process of David's script. Although Saul's actions were provoked by jealousy and evil, David recognized Saul's position of authority, and refused to lay a hand on him. That's why the bible tells us in ***1 Chronicles 16:22***, "Do not touch my anointed ones, and do my prophets no harm". That means, don't touch them with your mouth or your hands, even when you think they're wrong. Don't worry, if they are wrong, God will deal with them. That's *His* job, not yours. You just stick to the script, even when it looks like it's getting worse. Don't let anything or anyone, including yourself, pull you away from God.

Scripture points: ***(Philippians 3:14 NKJV) I press toward the goal for the prize of the upward call of God in Christ Jesus.***

(Romans 8:35 NKJV) Who shall separate us from the love of Christ? Shall tribulation, or distress, or persecution, or famine, or nakedness, or peril, or sword?

What would *your* answer to Paul's question be in ***Romans 8:35***? Can you honestly say that, no matter what, I will not separate myself from God? What about your own weapons? Will you suffer self-inflicted wounds? If you don't recognize your own weapons, you'll shoot yourself in the foot. Here are just a few of the weapons you may be using on yourself:

1) Jealousy ***(Ezekiel 8:5-6)***
2) Manipulation ***(Judges 16:15-16)***
3) Intimidation ***(1 Kings 19:2-3)***
4) Possessiveness/Territorialism ***(Acts 8:18-20)***
5) Gossip ***(Proverbs 11:13, 12:17)***
6) Low self-esteem ***(Jeremiah 1:6)***
7) Greed ***(Acts 5:1-4)***

8) Pride ***(James 4:6)***

9) Laziness ***(Proverbs 21:25)***

10) Procrastination ***(Acts 24:24-25)***

For these weapons are not weapons that people throw at you, but weapons you use to separate yourself from God. Examine your heart to make sure that these weapons are not in your arsenal. Endure the process, endure the pain, because in the end, you win.

***Scripture points:* (Psalm 30:5 NKJV) For His anger is but for a moment, His favor is for life; Weeping may endure for a night, but joy comes in the morning.**

(Romans 8:31 NKJV) What then shall we say to these things? If God is for us, who can be against us?

God is on your side. Just make sure you're on His side. You can go through the storm, because God is with you. He is working out His ultimate plan and purpose for your life. The storms, the battles, and even the weapons are ordained by God to push you to your full potential.

DON'T QUIT!

Prayer

Upon completion of this book, I am requesting that you recite this prayer aloud. Be encouraged and strengthened during your process leading to your purpose.

Dear God,

I recognize that You are my source. All that I am comes from You. I come to You repenting for every time I doubted the process of my purpose. Thank you for still choosing me through all of the doubt and fears I had. Lord, You are my strength in weak times, and a light unto my path. When I didn't acknowledge that I was fearfully and wonderfully made, You did Lord. Thank you for being patient with me. I want to be everything that You desire for me to be spiritually, emotionally, physically, socially, and financially. Thank you for revealing that most of my failures were not a result of the devil, but a result of my choices. This day I affirm to walk in the power of Your word. I declare that no weapon that is formed against me shall prosper, I am the head and not the tail, I am above only, and not beneath, and, I can do all things through Christ who strengthens me. I trust in Your word which also tells me that, if God be for me, no one can be against me, or separate me from Your love. Lord, please reveal my next assignment that is in conjunction with my purpose. Teach me to endure the process so I won't quit! Thank you for what You're going to do in me and through me. This is Your servant's prayer.

In Jesus' name, Amen.

NOTES

NOTES

ORDER THESE LIFE-CHANGING MESSAGES FROM PASTOR TONY SMITH TODAY!

Victory Ministries International
c/o VMI Media Ministry
807 E. 43rd Street
Baltimore, Maryland 21212
(410) 433-8066

or visit at

www.victorycenterministries.org

Available in audio and video cassette, CD and DVD

The bible teaches us that "...the one that endureth to the end shall be saved". These scriptures really come to life as Pastor Tony Smith uses a dramatic illustration to show that you can overcome the obstacles and the challenges that the enemy uses to tempt you to give up. You will be encouraged to endure!
Item #030501

This 14-part series will take you back to the beginning, back to God. Pastor Tony will walk you through the book of Genesis and show you how man lost his place of authority and dominion over the earth but how God had a plan to restore us back to our rightful place in Him. - *Item #020502*

Pastor Tony delivers this groundbreaking message with such practicality and gives biblically-based details on what a man needs to possess and what a woman should look for before entering into marriage. - *Item #050201*

God never promised that there would not be weapons formed to attack your purpose but He does assure you that they will not prosper and that in the end, you win! This message will encourage you to go through the storms and the battles for the Lord is on your side. - *Item #040501*

The bible teaches us that many are called but few are chosen. Those who are chosen understand that there is a God-designed process that they must go through before they can fully walk in their purpose. In this message, Pastor Tony explains the various things you may go through while you're in your process and gives you hope that God has ordained this and is with you every step of the way!
Item #040502